GREAT CLASSIC RECIPES OF EUROPE

Also by Sandy Lesberg

The Single Chef's Cookbook
Specialty of the House

Great Classic Recipes of Europe by Sandy Lesberg
Copyright 1972 in all countries of the International
Copyright Union by Sandy Lesberg
Prepared and produced by Rutledge Books, Inc.
All rights reserved. No part of this book may be
reproduced in any form or by any means, except for
the inclusion of brief quotations in a review, without
permission in writing from the publisher.
Library of Congress Catalog Card Number: 72-2311
ISBN: 0-13-36372-2
Printed in Italy by Mondadori, Verona
Prentice-Hall International, Inc., London
Prentice-Hall of Australia, Pty. Ltd., North Sydney
Prentice-Hall of Canada, Ltd., Toronto
Prentice-Hall of India Private Ltd., New Delhi
Prentice-Hall of Japan, Inc., Tokyo

GREAT CLASSIC RECIPES OF EUROPE

By Sandy Lesberg

Recipes from the finest European restaurants,
compiled with the cooperation of the American Express Money Card

PRENTICE-HALL, INC.
Englewood Cliffs, N. J.

This book is for Dewars and Harpo,
my once and future friends

INTRODUCTION

This is no ordinary cookbook.

For instance there's a broiled lobster recipe from a restaurant in Lyons, France, that includes chopped shallots, mashed truffle and cognac and is signed by Chef Marc Alix, indicating its pedigree. Our beet soup with dumplings recipe comes from Warsaw (The Europejski) and a steak tartare Maréchal Duroc is from the Hotel Napoléon in Paris. The beef Wellington is a triumph served regularly at the Kensington Palace Hotel in London.

In fact *all* the recipes in this unique collection are specialties of some of the most important restaurants in Europe. For many it is their first time in print. It's as if you invited the great chefs of the old world into your kitchen to let you in on the secrets of their favorite dishes; these are the recipes that make them the most prideful artists in the world.

The dishes that you think you recognize as old friends should be examined closely. Every chef relishes the idea of taking a well-known recipe and changing it just enough to put his personal stamp on it before sending it out of the kitchen. Take the minestrone soup from Malta, for instance. Maybe it's the ten raw eggs or the cottage cheese—something makes it different. And delicious. Or another way to prepare scampi—this time from the Fem Små Hus in Stockholm. Called Scampi Indiana, it involves among other exotic items curry and cognac. Obviously a challenge.

The book is not meant to be a primer in cooking. We have asked the chefs to give us their specialty recipes, which does not necessarily mean their easiest. But the kitchen is a place where ambitions and capacities can be stretched beyond all previous accomplishments. It is to be hoped that these pages will supply the impetus as well as the information necessary to help you refine your own cooking sophistication.

The fine professional organization of American Express approached these great restaurants with the idea of urging these chefs of outstanding skill and reputation to instruct us in the preparation of their favorite dishes presented in such a way as to allow even the most timid person in the kitchen a fair chance of accomplishing the most challenging recipe.

The cultural richness of a great many Americans as well as Europeans is firmly rooted in the foods of Europe. In many ways, then, this book is a return to the roots. It is also a grand way to be an armchair traveler by serving dishes from some of the most fascinating cities in the world. And for the more seasoned traveler—test your memory. Chances are that you can remember much of your journeying from the food you met along the way.

More and more men and women alike are turning to the kitchen as a palliative to the hectic existence of contemporary life. The more we are forced to cope with a strenuous world, the more important it is to discover a way to retain our sense of balance. Gourmet cooking serves many people as a magnificent means of achieving calm between the storms. As I said before, this is no ordinary cookbook. It represents the finest recipes of the finest chefs in Europe and is presented to you in the hope that it will afford you many peaceful moments in the preparation as well as many satisfying moments in the eating.

The chefs themselves have suggested wines to accompany the recipes. If you find any of them impossible to obtain or super-expensive, your local wine merchant will offer a first-class substitute.

CONTENTS

Section One

APPETIZERS

de Gravenmolen

Amsterdam, Netherlands

Chef: Alexander Koene

TERRINE DE RIS DE VEAU PISTACHE
(Sweetbreads Pâté with Pistachios)

 4 cups veal broth
 1 bay leaf
   Pinch rosemary
   Pinch thyme
 ¼ cup minced shallots
 1½ pounds (750 grams) blanched veal sweetbreads, diced
   Salt and freshly ground pepper to taste
 1 tablespoon brandy
 2 tablespoons dry white wine
 1¼ cups ground raw veal
 1¼ cups ground raw lean pork
 2 truffles, chopped
 ½ pound (250 grams) green bacon, sliced
   Sauce Cumberland (recipe follows)

Reduce veal broth by half with bay leaf, rosemary, thyme and shallots. Place sweetbreads in pan; season and flame with brandy. Add white wine. Mix thoroughly with veal, pork and truffles. Line a terrine with bacon, allowing slices to extend at the top. Fill terrine with mixed ingredients and fold ends of bacon slices over filling. Cook in oven au bain-marie (set in a pan of hot water) for 45 minutes. Serve with Sauce Cumberland and a Waldorf salad, if desired.

Sauce Cumberland

 2 shallots, minced
 1 lemon
 1 orange
 ¼ cup red currant jelly
 ¼ cup port
 1 teaspoon dry mustard
 ½ teaspoon cayenne
 1 teaspoon powdered ginger

Cook shallots in ¼ cup water until tender. Peel lemon and orange, and shred peel in fine strips. Parboil and drain. Juice the orange and lemon. Place in saucepan with all the other ingredients, including the cooked shallots, and heat until jelly is melted. Taste for seasonings. Serve hot or cold.

Serves: 4 to 6

Wine: Dry Loire or light red Bordeaux

Les Mésanges

Montbonnot (Isère), France

Chef: G. Achini

TERRINE DE FOIE GRAS FRAIS
(Mold of Fresh Goose Liver)

1 large goose liver
   Salt and freshly ground pepper to taste
½ cup port
1 tablespoon armagnac

Carefully trim goose liver, removing veins, and soak in 2 cups cold water for 30 minutes. Then wipe dry and season with salt and pepper. Put the liver in a small terrine (covered earthenware baking dish) and moisten with port and armagnac. Cover the terrine tightly. Let marinate for 2 hours.

To bake, place the terrine in a bain-marie and bake for 20 to 25 minutes in a moderate (350° F.) oven. Serve hot or cold directly from terrine as an appetizer or first course with crisp dry toast or crackers.

Serves: 8

Lamazere

Paris, France

Chef: Henri Ricottier

FOIE GRAS DANS SA ROBE NATURELLE ET TRUFFE
(Goose Liver as Prepared by Roger Lamazère)

1 large goose liver
1 tablespoon salt
1 teaspoon freshly ground pepper
   Goose fat
1 large black truffle* (optional)
1 slice bacon

Remove all inside veins from liver with a small knife. While it is open in two lobes, add salt and pepper. Close liver and wrap it in muslin so that it will keep its natural shape while cooking. Put it in a pan with enough goose fat so that the fat, when melted, reaches to three-quarters the height of the liver. Cook, keeping fat under the boiling point, about 30 minutes, or until the liver is very tender. When cooked, put it, still hot, on a rack so that the fat will drain. The liver will keep in the refrigerator for about two weeks.

To serve, slice thickly and garnish with sliced truffle if you wish.

Serves: 6

*The truffle season is short in France, stretching roughly from the middle of December to the end of February. The best way to cook a truffle is to roll it in a slice of bacon and then in a piece of aluminum foil. Cook it 20 minutes in wood embers or in a hot oven.

Wine: Sauterne or champagne

Hunting Lodge
London, England
Chef: H. P. Lullier

HUNTING LODGE PATE

2 pounds (1 kilogram) belly of pork
1 pound (500 grams) neck of pork
2 cups lean veal or game, according to season
4 slices green bacon
½ cup chicken livers
1 teaspoon freshly ground white pepper
   Salt to taste
1 teaspoon sweet paprika
½ teaspoon ground cloves
½ teaspoon fresh thyme
1 tablespoon sugar
1 teaspoon saltpeter
¼ cup brandy
¼ cup Madeira
3 eggs
½ cup unflavored dry gelatin, softened in 1 cup cold water
1 tablespoon arrowroot or cornstarch
½ cup mango chutney

1 bramley (tart) apple, chopped
2 tablespoons larding fat, cut into small cubes
½ cup chopped shallots
1 pound (500 grams) larding fat, sliced thin

Chop first five ingredients into 1-inch cubes. Marinate 24 hours in a mixture of the pepper, salt, paprika, cloves, thyme, sugar, saltpeter, brandy and Madeira; then grind the meats through the fine blade of a food mill. Mix in eggs, softened gelatin, arrowroot or cornstarch, mango chutney, apple, 2 tablespoons larding fat and shallots. Line a large terrine with slices of larding fat, leaving ends outside terrine. Place pâté mixture in terrine and press down firmly. Fold ends of fat slices over top of pâté to completely enclose. Place terrine in a bath of simmering water and bake, covered tightly, for about 2 hours in a moderately slow (300° F.) oven. Test for doneness by inserting a cake tester in the center of the pâté; it should come out clean. Let cool in terrine. Chill if pâté is not to be used at once. Serve with melba toast and crackers, if desired.

Serves: 24

Aubette
Strasbourg, France
Chef: J. P. Offenburger

FOIE D'OIE FRAIS D'ALSACE AUX POMMES DE REINETTE

(Fresh Alsatian Goose Liver with Apples)

 1 goose liver
 ¼ cup cognac
 ¼ cup Madeira
   Salt and freshly ground pepper to taste
   Pinch thyme
 1 bay leaf
   Salt and freshly ground pepper to taste
 ¼ cup flour
 ¼ cup butter
 2 tablespoons butter
 ½ cup light brown sugar
 ½ cup peeled, cored and sliced (crosswise) apples

Carefully devein goose liver and soak for 24 hours in cognac, Madeira, salt, pepper, thyme and bay leaf.

Dry liver and cut into medium-sized slices; season with salt and pepper and dredge in flour. Cook in ¼ cup hot butter until lightly browned.

Melt the 2 tablespoons butter and brown the sugar in a small skillet. Add apple slices and turn carefully to coat with caramel until the apples are almost tender. Add a tablespoon of boiling water if syrup hardens before apples are done.

Arrange liver slices on a platter and garnish with rounds of candied apples.

Serves: 4

Wine: Tokay d'Alsace

Jalta
Prague, Czechoslovakia
Chef: M. Jirasek

XAVEROV

(Cold Hors d'Oeuvres)

 2 small stewed chickens
 ½ cup mayonnaise
 1 tablespoon lemon juice
 4 small slices ham
 1¼ cups heavy cream, whipped
 4 sprigs parsley
   Lettuce leaves
 8 canned or brandied peach halves
 1 lemon, sliced

Remove chicken meat from the bones and cut into pieces (there should be about 3 cups of meat). Add mayonnaise and lemon juice. Refrigerate until ready to serve. Prepare ham cornets for garnish by shaping ham slices inside small pointed paper cups. Chill. When ready to serve, fill ham cornets with unsweetened whipped cream and decorate with parsley.

To serve, arrange lettuce leaves on individual plates. Place two peach halves on each plate and heap them with chicken salad. Remove ham from cups and arrange on plate with lemon slices to garnish. Serve very cold.

Serves: 4

Restaurant de la Mère Guy

Lyon, France

Chef: Roger Roucou

L'OREILLER DE LA BELLE AURORE

("Pillow of the Beautiful Morning Sun")

2 pheasants
1 cup cubed veal
1¼ cups cubed fresh pork
1¼ cups pork fat
   Salt and freshly ground pepper to taste
1 tablespoon minced dried mushrooms
1 tablespoon cognac
½ teaspoon salt
2½ cups flour
1 cup shortening
½ cup quartered fresh truffles
½ cup fresh foie gras, sliced
1 egg yolk, beaten
1 truffle, finely minced
1 cup Madeira Sauce (see index)

Bone pheasants and set aside fillets of meat. Cut fillets into strips. Finely grind the liver of the pheasant with the pheasant skin, the veal, the pork and pork fat. Season this stuffing with salt, pepper, mushrooms and cognac.

Make pastry by sifting salt with flour and then cutting cold shortening into it. Add ½ cup cold water a tablespoon at a time until dough holds its shape. Divide in half. Roll out half the pastry in a strip. Place on it half the stuffing. On top of this, arrange the strips of pheasant fillets in a band. Over this lay quarters of truffles and sliced foie gras. Cover with the rest of the stuffing and close up with another band of the flaky pastry. The result will look like a pillow.

Place pillow on a baking sheet and brush the top of the pastry with the beaten egg yolk. Prick two or three holes to allow the steam to escape. Bake it in a moderately hot (375° F.) oven for 35 to 40 minutes. Heat minced truffle gently in Madeira Sauce for 10 minutes and serve with very hot pâté en croute.

Serves: 6

Wine: Musigny Conte de Vogue

Hotel National

Moscow, Soviet Union

FISH HORS D'OEUVRE

2 hard-cooked eggs, peeled and cut in half lengthwise
1 tablespoon finely minced smoked sevruga*
1 tablespoon finely minced smoked beluga*
1 tablespoon butter
1 teaspoon lemon juice
2 tablespoons black or red caviar
   Salad greens
1 cucumber
1 tomato

Carefully remove egg yolks and mash. Mix well with smoked fish, butter and lemon juice. Carefully fold in caviar. Try to break the caviar as little as possible. Pile yolk mixture back into egg-white shells. Serve on plates lined with salad greens and decorated with sliced cucumber and tomato.

Serves: 2

*Sturgeonlike fish native to the Caspian and Black seas. If your delicatessen or gourmet food store does not stock these delicacies, smoked whitefish or smoked salmon is a suitable substitute.

Section Two

SOUPS

Grand

Warsaw, Poland

KRUPNIK POLSKI ZABIELANY

(White Groat Soup)

½ cup barley groats
2 tablespoons butter
2¼ cups peeled diced potatoes
4½ cups veal or chicken consommé
1 cup heavy cream
2½ tablespoons salt
2 tablespoons finely chopped dillweed
1 tablespoon finely chopped parsley

Wash the groats in several changes of cold water. Pour 4½ cups boiling water over the groats, add butter and boil slowly, covered, until the groats are separate and tender. Boil potatoes separately. Put the groats and boiled potatoes into hot consommé; add cream and season with salt. Sprinkle with dillweed and parsley, and serve very hot.

Serves: 10

La Poularde

Nice, France

Chef: Joseph

SOUPE DE POISSONS

(Fish Soup)

2 medium onions, sliced
2 leeks (white portions only), sliced
6 tablespoons olive oil
3 tomatoes, peeled and crushed
1 clove garlic
Pinch fresh or dried fennel
2 pounds (1 kilogram) small firm-fleshed fish
½ teaspoon salt
½ teaspoon pepper
Saffron threads
4 slices bread, lightly toasted
1 clove garlic, halved
Grated Parmesan cheese

Cook the onion and leek in hot olive oil until golden brown. Add tomatoes, garlic and fennel. In the meantime, wash and clean small fish (it is not necessary to gut so-called rock fish), place them in prepared mixture; cover with 1 cup water. Add salt and pepper and saffron; cook on high flame for 30 minutes. Strain mixture through a vegetable strainer (fine mesh). Rub dried bread lightly with halved garlic clove and use as a base for boiling hot soup. Sprinkle with Parmesan cheese and serve.

Serves: 4

Wine: Rosé de Provence

Le Relais, Cafe Royal
London, England
Chef: G. Mouilleron

SOUPE DE POISSON MARSEILLAISE

(Fish Soup Marseillaise)

¼ cup olive oil
½ cup chopped celery
¾ cup sliced onion
2 cloves garlic, chopped
1¼ cups quartered ripe tomatoes
   Pinch saffron
1 cup coarsely diced weever fish*
1 cup coarsely diced angler fish*
¾ cup coarsely diced John Dory fish*
¾ cup coarsely diced red mullet*
¼ cup shelled prawns
   Salt and freshly ground pepper to taste
1 cup peeled, diced potatoes
1 red pepper, cut up
1 tablespoon soaked white bread crumbs
   Rouille (recipe follows)

Pour oil into a large pan, warm slightly, add celery and onion and cook until onion becomes translucent. Stir in garlic for a minute or so; then add the rest of the ingredients, except Rouille, and 7 cups water. Boil for 1 hour. Retrieve as many of the fish bones as possible and then strain soup through a fine sieve. Garnish with fried bread spread with Rouille.

Rouille

1 tablespoon white bread crumbs
1 tablespoon milk
2 cloves garlic
1 red pepper, cut up
   Salt and freshly ground pepper to taste
¼ cup olive oil
   Fried bread

Soak bread crumbs in milk. Pound garlic with red pepper and bread crumbs. Season with salt and pepper. Very slowly mix in olive oil, beating constantly. Spread on fried bread.

Serves: 6

*Or equivalent quantity assorted flatfish.

Wine: Old Trinity House Madeira

Pagoda

Madrid, Spain

Chef: Chien Soi Shien

SHARK'S FIN WITH CHICKEN BROTH

1 pound (500 grams) soaked* short shark's fin
2 stalks spring onion
3 tablespoons dry white wine
9 cups chicken stock
¼ cup peanut oil
1 pound (500 grams) cooked chicken, shredded
½ cup Chinese mushrooms, soaked and shredded
1 cup bamboo shoots, cooked and cut in strips
3 tablespoons soy sauce
2 tablespoons salt
1 teaspoon sugar
6 tablespoons cornstarch, mixed with 6 tablespoons water
2 tablespoons shredded cooked ham
¼ teaspoon freshly ground black pepper

Put the prepared shark's fin in a pan with 3 cups of cold water, a stalk of spring onion and 2 tablespoons wine and cook for 10 minutes over low heat. Drain off the water. Add 3 cups chicken stock to the same pan, cook another 10 minutes over low heat, remove shark's fin and discard this soup.

Heat oil in frying pan, stir in the remaining spring onion stalk, quickly sprinkle in one tablespoon wine and add 6 cups chicken stock. Add shredded chicken, Chinese mushrooms, bamboo shoots and shark's fin. Let this boil, season with soy sauce, salt and sugar; then thicken with cornstarch mixture. Pour into a big soup bowl, sprinkle with shredded ham and black pepper and serve.

Serves: 4 to 6

*Shark's fin should be soaked in 6 cups cold water for 2 hours, then simmered in the soaking water for about half an hour over low heat and allowed to cool. The water should be discarded and the procedure repeated. One-quarter pound dried shark's fin will yield one pound softened shark's fin.

Sadko Restaurant

Leningrad, Soviet Union

RASSOLNIK

½ cup peeled, diced potato
½ cup diced onions
¼ cup chopped tart cucumber pickles
¼ cup diced celery
  Salt to taste
  Spices to taste (a nice selection might be ½ teaspoon each oregano, basil and dillweed)
½ cup 1-inch pieces sturgeon fillet or salmon steak
½ cup 1-inch pieces trout or other firm freshwater fish fillet
2 sprigs parsley, chopped

Cook potato, onion, pickle, celery, salt and spices in 3 cups briskly boiling water for 20 minutes, or until the potato is almost tender. Add sturgeon, trout and parsley. Simmer very gently for about 10 minutes, or until fish flakes easily. Do not overcook.

Serves: 3 or 4

Athénée Palace

Bucharest, Romania

Chef: Constantin Tutila

ROMANIAN VEAL SOUP

1¾ pounds (875 grams) veal shoulder

4½ pounds (2.25 kilograms) veal bones

1 tablespoon olive oil

3¼ cups julienne carrots

1¾ cups julienne parsnips

1¼ cups julienne celery

1¼ cups julienne white cabbage

1¼ cups julienne green pepper

1¼ cups minced onion

1¼ cups green beans

1¼ cups peas

2 egg yolks

1 cup heavy cream

½ cup lemon juice

   Salt and freshly ground white pepper to taste

1½ tablespoons minced parsley

Place veal and bones in large saucepan with enough water to cover and simmer for about 1 hour.

Heat oil in a very large saucepan. In it place all the julienne vegetables and the onion. Cover and simmer over low heat for 10 to 15 minutes, or until vegetables are soft but not brown. Set aside.

Blanch beans and peas separately. Set aside.

Whip egg yolks and cream together until well blended and slightly thick. Set aside.

Remove meat from cooking liquid and strain. Return meat and strained liquid to the pan, and add all the vege-tables. Simmer for 15 minutes. Remove from heat; mix in lemon juice. Add egg-yolk-and-cream mixture. Season to taste. Sprinkle the top with minced parsley.

Serves: 6

Malta Hilton

Malta

SOPPA TAL-ARMLA

(Maltese Minestrone)

¼ cup yellow split peas

2 tablespoons finely chopped onion

1 cup oil

½ cup diced celery

1 cup diced carrots

¼ cup diced cauliflower

¼ cup diced red or white cabbage

1½ cups peeled, diced potatoes

2 tablespoons tomato paste

   Salt and freshly ground pepper to taste

10 eggs

½ cup cottage cheese

Presoak split peas in 1 cup water; then boil until they are almost cooked. Fry the onion until limp in the oil in a very large pan. Add the rest of the vegetables and lightly brown. Stir in tomato paste and ½ cup water; and then add split peas and cook for approximately 40 minutes, or until all the vegetables are well cooked. Season to taste.

To serve, place soup in individual casserole dishes, and bring to boil. Into each dish break an egg and poach it. Then sprinkle with cottage cheese. Serve very hot.

Serves: 10

Hotel National

Moscow, Soviet Union

MOSCOW BORSCH

½ cup shredded cabbage
2 sprigs parsley
3 cups meat broth
¼ cup diced beets
¼ cup diced carrots
¼ cup diced onion
2 tablespoons butter
  Salt and freshly ground pepper to taste
1 bay leaf
1 tablespoon sugar
½ cup ground beef
½ cup diced raw or cooked ham
2 tablespoons flour (optional)
  Sour cream or unsweetened whipped cream
  Chopped fennel

Cook cabbage and parsley in meat broth for ½ hour. Meanwhile sauté beets, carrots and onion in butter. Add to broth. Season with salt, pepper, bay leaf and sugar. Lightly brown ground beef and ham; add to soup and simmer for 2 hours. Stir frequently. The soup may be thickened by mixing flour with ¼ cup cold water and stirring in 10 minutes before soup is finished cooking. (The flour must be thoroughly cooked.)

Top each serving with a dollop of sour cream or unsweetened whipped cream and a sprinkling of chopped fennel. Cheesecake is the traditional dessert.

Serves: 4

Five Flies

Amsterdam, Netherlands

BISQUE OF SMOKED EEL

1 smoked eel
¼ cup butter
¼ cup chopped onion
2 peppercorns
1 bay leaf
1 tablespoon tomato purée
2 tablespoons flour
4 cups fish stock
  Salt and freshly ground pepper to taste
1 tablespoon dry white wine
1 teaspoon Worcestershire sauce
1 tablespoon heavy cream

Skin, bone and cut up eel; reserve. Melt butter in saucepan; add eel meat, bone and skin. Toss for few minutes before adding onion, peppercorns and bay leaf. Add tomato purée, flour and finally the stock. Boil until eel is well cooked; then pass the mixture through a fine sieve, rubbing with wooden spoon. Season with salt and pepper, white wine and Worcestershire sauce. Finish bisque with cream. Serve very hot.

Serves: 2

Grand

Warsaw, Poland

BIGOS STAROPOLSKI

(Old Polish Hunter's Stew)

4½ cups sauerkraut
  3 cups finely shredded white cabbage
2¼ cups diced smoked bacon
2¼ cups crumbled Polish sausage
1¼ cups pork, removed from spareribs or chops
  3 tablespoons salt
 ¼ teaspoon freshly ground pepper
  1 clove garlic, minced
 ¼ teaspoon marjoram
 ⅛ teaspoon paprika
  1 cup chopped onions
 ¼ cup lard
  3 tablespoons flour
 ½ cup pitted prunes
 ½ cup tomato paste
 ½ cup Madeira

Heat sauerkraut. Cook cabbage in water barely to cover just until limp. Fry bacon and sausage; add pork to skillet and cook gently until tender. Combine meats with sauerkraut and cabbage in a large stew pot; add salt, pepper, garlic, marjoram and paprika. Sauté onion in the lard. Stir in flour and cook until golden. Add to the bigos. Cook, covered, a minimum of 3 hours. Cook the prunes and, before serving stew, add prunes, tomato paste and Madeira. Bigos is served with bread only.

Serves: 10

Wine: Polish vodka Wyborowa or dry red wine

Restaurant de Boerdery

Amsterdam, Netherlands

Chef: H. F. Wunneberg

CONSOMME LADY CURZON

 1 tablespoon butter
 2 tablespoons curry powder
 1 tablespoon brandy
 ½ cup heavy cream
 4 cups clear turtle soup

Melt the butter with curry powder. Flame with brandy. Add turtle soup and cream. Serve very hot in small cups.

Serves: 4 to 6

Restaurant Gundel

Budapest, Hungary

Chef: Julius Pár

UJHAZI'S CHICKEN BROTH

  1 3-pound (1.5-kilogram) fowl
  2 carrots
  2 parsnips
¼ cup chopped celery
  2 tablespoons chopped onion
  1 clove garlic
½ cup mushrooms
  1 green pepper, seeded and quartered
1½ tablespoons salt
  5 peppercorns
  2 tablespoons tomato purée
½ cup flour
  1 egg

Clean, draw and wash fowl. Put in 8 cups salted water and boil, together with carrots, parsnips, celery, onion, garlic, mushrooms, green pepper, salt, peppercorns and tomato purée, until fowl is tender. Strain. Reserve the vegetables.

Mix flour and egg; knead the dough until smooth. Roll thin and cut into thin slices. Let noodles dry a few minutes before boiling until tender in the strained soup. Slice the cooked carrots, parsnips and mushrooms; add to soup and serve hot.

Serves: 5

Wine: Chablis or beer

Sadko Restaurant

Leningrad, Soviet Union

BORSCH

  1 teaspoon salt
    Freshly ground pepper to taste
½ cup sliced mushrooms
½ cup sliced carrots
½ cup diced onions
½ cup sauerkraut
  2 sprigs parsley
  2 strips green bacon, cut in 1-inch pieces
½ cup sour cream
  2 tablespoons butter
  2 tablespoons tomato paste

Put 3 cups water, salt, pepper, mushrooms, carrots, onion, sauerkraut, parsley and bacon in a heavy pan. Cook slowly for 1 to 1½ hours (check carrots for tenderness). Reduce heat still further and add sour cream, butter, tomato paste; taste for seasonings. After the sour cream has been added, the soup must not boil. Stir frequently as soup thickens, about 10 minutes.

Serves: 4

Europejski

Warsaw, Poland

BARSZCZ Z USZKAMI

(Beet Soup with Dumplings)

4¼ cups peeled, sliced beets
1 cup mixed chopped vegetables (celery, onions, carrots, etc.)
1 bay leaf
1 clove garlic
2 tablespoons vinegar
1 tablespoon salt
¼ teaspoon sugar
   Freshly ground pepper to taste
   Dumplings (recipe follows)

Cook beets in 8 cups water with vegetables, bay leaf and garlic until vegetables are tender. Strain the broth and season with vinegar, salt, sugar and pepper. Discard the vegetables. Make Dumplings, add to soup and serve.

Dumplings

1½ cups flour
1 tablespoon salt
1 egg
1 cup ground seasoned cooked meat or deviled ham or cooked, drained sausage

Sift the flour with salt into a bowl. Add 6 tablespoons water and the egg. Knead until dough is smooth. Roll out on a lightly floured surface. Cut into 2-inch squares. Place a teaspoon of the meat in the center of each square and fold over to form a triangle. Seal edges. Cook in salted boiling water for 12 minutes.

Serves: 10

Parc des Eaux-Vives

Geneva, Switzerland

Chef: Ido Viale

VELOUTE OCEANE

(Ocean Soup)

1 cup dry white wine
¼ cup minced shallots
4 sprigs parsley
1 sprig thyme
½ bay leaf
   Salt and freshly ground white pepper to taste
12 mussels in shells
6 egg yolks
¼ cup heavy cream
   Salt to taste
   Cayenne
   Crushed dry chervil

Put the wine into a large saucepan with shallots; add the parsley, thyme, bay leaf, ¼ cup water, salt and pepper. Cook 4 or 5 minutes. Add the mussels and cover the pan. Cook just until mussels are opened. (Discard any that do not open.) Set mussels aside. Strain the soup and keep it very hot.

Mix the egg yolks and the cream with a little of the hot soup. Return egg-cream mixture to soup, stirring vigorously while it thickens. Do not allow soup to boil after eggs are added. Season with salt and cayenne to taste.

Shell mussels and sprinkle with chervil. Serve soup and accompanying mussels very hot.

Serves: 4

Grand Hotel Royal
Stockholm, Sweden
Chef: Harry Westkämper

FRESH MUSSEL SOUP
WITH SHRIMPS

  1 tablespoon chopped celery
  1 tablespoon chopped carrot
  1 tablespoon chopped onion
  2 tablespoons olive oil
 20 fresh mussels in shells, well washed
  2 cups fish stock
  1 tablespoon chopped white of leek
  1 teaspoon saffron threads
 ½ teaspoon garlic powder
 ¼ cup butter
 ¼ cup heavy cream
  1 egg yolk
  2 tomatoes
  2 tablespoons butter
 ¼ cup shelled cooked shrimp
  1 cup dry white wine
  1 tablespoon chopped parsley
    Salt and freshly ground white pepper to
    taste

Sauté celery, carrot and onion in olive oil in large pot. Add mussels and fish stock. Boil until mussels have opened. (Discard any that do not open.) Remove mussels and separate from shells. Sauté the leek, saffron and garlic in ¼ cup butter. Add mussel broth and boil for about 12 minutes. Thicken stock with cream and egg yolk.

Peel and seed tomatoes; chop and sauté in 2 tablespoons butter. When tomatoes have lost most of their liquid and are quite thick (this will take some time), add mussels, shrimp and wine. Simmer just to heat through. Do not boil or shellfish will become tough. Add the boiling hot soup and chopped parsley. Season to taste with salt and white pepper.

Serves: 4

Wine: Dopff Riquewihr, Domaines Dopff

Section Three

GAME AND GAME BIRDS

Savoy Hotel
Malmö, Sweden
Chef: Einar Petersson

FILLET OF REINDEER MARINATED WITH JUNIPER BERRIES

  1 3-pound (1.5-kilogram) fillet of reindeer
¼ cup butter
  2 cups strong reindeer stock
  1 cup dry red wine
  1 cup salad oil
  1 tablespoon crushed dried juniper berries
    Salt and freshly ground pepper to taste
  1 tablespoon arrowroot
  1 teaspoon gin
  1 teaspoon soy sauce (optional)
    Sautéed Apples (recipe follows)

Bone the fillet from the saddle. Break the saddle bone into small pieces and brown well in butter in a roasting pan. Add 1 cup water, bring to boil and simmer for stock. Immerse fillet in a mixture of wine, oil and juniper berries and marinate overnight. Remove fillet from marinade, dry it, reserve marinade.

Salt and pepper meat and broil for 15 to 20 minutes in roasting pan. When meat is ready, take out and wrap in foil to keep warm.

Stir the stock and skim. Mix in the marinade and thicken with arrowroot that has been mixed with a little water. Add gin and boil until sauce is dark brown. If soy sauce is added to improve color, put it in a little at a time, tasting carefully.

Slice meat, preferably at a 45° angle, and place on dish. Pour on half the sauce; serve remainder in sauce bowl. Serve with Sautéed Apples and pommes Dauphine, if desired.

Sautéed Apples

  2 cups sliced apples, peeled
1½ tablespoons butter
  6 tablespoons heavy cream
  1 tablespoon armagnac or cognac

Sauté the apple slices in butter. Add cream and simmer until soft. Place apples in serving dish. Add armagnac or cognac to cream and pour sauce over apples.

Serves: 4 to 6

Wine: Château Beauregard, Pomerol 1960

Le Petit Bedon
Paris, France
Chef: Jacques Tiéc

CUISSOT DE MARCASSIN OU CHEVREUIL SAUCE VENAISON

(Quarter of Young Wild Boar or Venison)

  1 6-pound (3-kilogram) quarter boar or
    venison
  1 fifth dry red wine
    Bones from game, if available, or beef, veal
    or pork bones
  1 large onion, sliced
  2 large carrots, sliced
1½ tablespoons chopped parsley
  1 teaspoon thyme
10 peppercorns
  1 tablespoon vinegar
    Salt and freshly ground pepper to taste
  ¼ cup flour
  ¼ cup butter
  ½ cup sugar
  1 teaspoon vingar
  ½ cup heavy cream
    Salt and freshly ground pepper to taste
  1 tablespoon red currant jelly
  1 cup whole or puréed chestnuts

Marinate quarter of game for 48 hours in next eight ingredients. Add no salt. When meat is ready to cook, remove from marinade and dry thoroughly with paper towels. Rub lightly all over with salt and pepper. Preheat oven to very hot (450° F.). Roast game for 20 minutes, then reduce heat to moderately slow (325° F.). Cook from 15 to 20 minutes per pound, depending on degree of doneness desired. When meat is done, remove from the oven and let stand 20 minutes before serving.

While meat is roasting, make game stock: Strain marinade. Brown bones, vegetables and seasonings in a heavy casserole. Pour liquid over browned vegetables and cook 1 hour, skimming off fat and foam frequently. Strain stock. In a saucepan, prepare brown roux of flour and butter, and add to game stock. Simmer, stirring with a wire whisk to avoid scorching, until thickened.

Carmelize sugar and vinegar. Pour into the sauce. Add cream. Season with salt and pepper and cook 20 minutes. Add red currant jelly, check seasonings and strain.

Arrange meat on a serving platter with whole or puréed chestnuts. Pour the sauce over meat and pass extra sauce.

Serves: 12

Wine: Burgundy (Richebourg Corton)

RISTORANTE ROSATI
Rome, Italy
Chef: Simioli
Costolette di Vitello "Rosati"
(page 97)

GRAND SOFIA
Sofia, Bulgaria
Chef: Velko Pavlov
Beef Fillet "Vreteno"
(page 89)

THE RUSSELL
Dublin, Ireland
Chef: Jackie Needham
Chicken Chaud-Froid
(page 73)

Rôtisserie des Cordeliers

Nancy, France

Chef: M. Antoine

CUISSOT DE CHEVREUIL FLORIDA
(Quarter of Deer)

- **2 deer quarters**
- **1 cup sliced carrots**
- **1 cup onions**
- **Bouquet Garni (see index)**
- **1 clove**
- **½ cup juniper berries**
- **Crushed peppercorns**
- **1 cup strong red wine**
- **¼ cup juniper berries**
- **Thyme**
- **¼ cup flour**
- **¼ cup cognac**
- **½ cup red currant jelly**
- **1 cup heavy cream**
- **Salt and freshly ground pepper to taste**

Bone deer quarters and tie them with string. Make a marinade with the next seven ingredients and the bones and trimmings of the deer. After eight days take out quarters, bones and trimmings and drain them well. Brown bones and trimmings in a roasting pan in a hot (400° F.) oven, adding ¼ cup juniper berries mixed with thyme. Add the marinade and a little flour to thicken to the pan in order to obtain the venison stock.

Roast the quarters, but keep them pink. Add the berry-and-thyme mixture. Deglaze roasting pan with cognac and red currant jelly. Strain the venison stock and add it to the pan. Then add cream and boil down the liquid to a mellow consistency. Check the seasoning.

To serve: Garnish meat platter with baked apples, purée of celery and purée of chestnuts, if desired. Serve sauce separately.

Serves: 10

Wine: Romanée Saint Vivant 1964

Wärdshuset Stallmästergården

Stockholm, Sweden

Chef: Walter Wirz

REINDEER CHOPS TORE WRITMAN

- **8 chops or medallions of young reindeer**
- **Salt and freshly ground pepper to taste**
- **½ cup flour**
- **¼ cup butter**
- **1 cup juniper berries, pounded**
- **¼ cup peeled, diced apple**
- **¾ cup heavy cream**
- **1 tablespoon butter**
- **2 cups fresh noodles**

Pound chops to flatten; season with salt and pepper. Dredge chops in flour; sauté in ¼ cup butter. When chops are almost done, add the juniper berries and the diced apple. Cook for 3 or 4 minutes; then add the cream and let it reduce by half. Season to taste and add 1 tablespoon of butter. Serve immediately with freshly made, hot noodles.

Serves: 4

Jalta

Prague, Czechoslovakia

Chef: M. Jirasek

VENISON JOINT "KONOPISTE CASTEL"

1 2-pound (1-kilogram) venison roast

¼ cup butter

1 onion, chopped

1 carrot, chopped

2 tomatoes

3 tablespoons cranberries

1 bay leaf

3 cups red wine

6 tablespoons Madeira Sauce (see index)
   Salt and freshly ground pepper to taste

8 small pears
   Butter

1 teaspoon cinnamon

1 tablespoon sugar

1 tablespoon rum

2 cups braised chestnuts

Sauté venison roast in butter together with onion and carrot. When meat is browned, add tomatoes, cranberries, bay leaf and 2½ cups wine. Cover and simmer until meat is very tender. Set roast aside and keep warm. Strain braising liquid and reduce by half to a thick gravy.

Add to the gravy the Madeira Sauce and the rest of the wine. (To make the gravy very smooth, add an additional small piece of butter.) Season with salt and pepper.

Cut the venison into slices and pour the gravy over it. Stew pears in butter with cinnamon and sugar. Garnish venison slices with pears and chestnuts, flame with rum and serve very hot.

Serves: 4

Wine: Heavy red Burgundy

Bingley Arms
Bardsey, Leeds, England
Chefs: Ian Walker and Christopher Haw

PHEASANT

(Recipe Dates from about 1750)

- **1 young pheasant**
- **2 cups red Chambertin wine**
- **¼ cup chopped carrots**
- **12 tiny onions**
- **2 bay leaves**
- **2 peppercorns**
- **¼ cup flour**
  Butter
- **12 mushroom caps**
- **4 lardons (fatty strips) of ham**
- **1 cup game or chicken stock**
  Salt and freshly ground pepper to taste
- **¼ teaspoon rosemary**
- **¼ teaspoon marjoram**
- **½ teaspoon chopped parsley**
- **1 large onion**

Pluck, draw and clean a young pheasant that has been hung for a period determined by personal taste. (If you buy your pheasant instead of shooting it, these steps will have been done by the vendor.) Cut the bird into two legs and two breasts and marinate for 6 to 8 hours (turning several times) in red Chambertin to which has been added carrots, onions, bay leaves and peppercorns. Remove pheasant and strain juices to use later for sauce.

Lightly flour the pheasant. Sauté very quickly in butter until lightly browned. Remove from pan. Place onions, mushroom caps and lardons of ham in pan and sauté these with light sprinkling of flour for about 2 minutes over a hot flame.

Drain surplus butter from the pan. Add strained Chambertin marinade and bring to boil. Add stock. Correct seasoning with salt and pepper and add rosemary, marjoram and parsley. Remove from flame.

Prepare earthenware or other unglazed casserole dish by soaking it in cold water. Rub outside with an onion to prevent its contracting and make sure the outside of vessel is dry before putting it in oven. Place pheasant pieces in casserole and add onions, mushrooms, lardons of ham and sauce. Allow to cook for 2 hours in a moderate (350° F.) oven. Serve straight from the casserole.

Serves: 2 to 4

Wine: Chambertin

Hotel Darroze

Villeneuve-de-Marsan, France

Chef: Claude Darroze

BALLOTINE DE FAISAN VILLENEUVOISE FLANQUEE D'ORTOLANS

(Pheasant Presented in Sausage Form, Garnished with Game Birds)

1 male pheasant
   Seasoned salt
1 tablespoon armagnac
1 cup coarsely chopped breast of fresh pork
1 cup coarsely chopped poultry meat
1 cup coarsely chopped ham
1 egg, beaten
½ cup pieces of larding bacon
   Salt and freshly ground pepper to taste
2 pounds (1 kilogram) veal and beef bones
½ cup Mirepoix (see index)
½ cup crushed tomatoes
   Bouquet Garni (see index)
1 clove garlic
½ cup pine nuts
1 cup butter
   Salt and freshly ground pepper to taste
1 fresh goose liver
2 tablespoons lemon juice
1 tablespoon armagnac
6 artichoke hearts
1 cup 1-inch asparagus pieces
1 thin slice ham (optional)
1 cup tiny new onions
1 cup peas
   Butter
1 cup mushrooms
   Butter
1 medium onion
1 cup dry white wine
1 cup white meat stock
6 ortolans*

Fat
Salt to taste
6 flaky pastry tart shells
6 puff-paste tart shells

Hang pheasant for at least 15 days. Cut off the neck, head, wings and tail and carefully pluck all parts of it. Reserve the skin, liver and gizzard; bone and devein the flesh. Reserve the carcass. Dice the meat and sprinkle it with seasoned salt. Moisten with armagnac and let it marinate several hours.

Chop meats, the pheasant trimmings, liver and gizzard and combine with pork, poultry meat and ham. Mix this stuffing with the marinated pheasant meat, the egg and the pieces of larding bacon. Season with salt and pepper. Line a rectangular mold with the skin of the pheasant and pack meat mixture into it. Place in a moderate (350° F.) oven in a pan of hot water and let it cook for 2 hours. (This preparation can be made 24 hours in advance. Keep very cold after cooking. This way the ballotine can be more easily cut with a knife.)

Place the veal and beef bones, the pheasant carcass cut into pieces and the mirepoix in a baking dish and cover with water. Add crushed tomatoes, Bouquet Garni and garlic. Let simmer in a slow (250° F.) oven for 2 hours. Prepare a brown roux with liver fat and pour the reduced stock over it. Strain stock through a fine mesh sieve and add pine nuts and butter. Season.

Salt and pepper the goose liver and steam it for 45 minutes with lemon juice and 1 tablespoon armagnac. Slice it and keep it warm.

Cook artichoke hearts. Stir-fry asparagus with a little sliced ham, if desired. Cook onions and peas together just until done; dress with butter.

Clean mushrooms. Sauté caps quickly in butter and set aside. Chop the stems and one medium onion. Sauté in the butter until tender. Add the mushroom caps, white wine and white meat stock. Cook gently until liquid is almost evaporated, about 1 hour.

Braise ortolans 5 minutes in fat. Salt and arrange them in individual flaky pastry tart shells.

Bake puff-paste tart shells in a hot (400° F.) oven until done.

Place the ballotine on a very large, long platter. In a puff-paste shell, place a slice of ballotine and over it a slice of goose liver. Rim the platter with alternating artichoke hearts stuffed with goose liver, ortolans in tart shells and filled puff-paste shells. At one end of the platter, leave space to place the remaining ballotine molded into the shape of a pheasant using the cooked cut-off parts. Sauce and mushrooms should be passed separately. Serve very hot.

Serves: 6

*Tiny birds (buntings) much prized as delicacies in Europe. Gourmet stores sometimes carry the small birds canned, or halves of very small Cornish hens could be used as a substitute.

Wine: Château la Lagure (Medoc) 1964

Swarte Schaep
Amsterdam, Netherlands
Chef: L. Lauterslager

FAISAN A L'ALSACIENNE

(Alsatian Pheasant)

- 2 2-pound (1-kilogram) pheasants
- ¼ cup butter
- ¼ cup peppercorns
- 2 tablespoons cognac
- 4 cups sauerkraut
- 1½ cups dry white wine
- 6 slices pineapple, cut in chunks
- 4 small smoked sausages
- 4 cups peeled, diced potatoes
- ½ cup heavy cream
- ¼ cup butter
- Nutmeg
- Salt to taste
- 1 cup boiled ham strips

Clean pheasants and sauté in butter with peppercorns until browned. Pour in warmed cognac and flame. Cover casserole and simmer pheasants in a slow (250° F.) oven until very tender. Heat sauerkraut in white wine. Mix in pineapple chunks, add sausages and keep warm. Boil potatoes until cooked. Mash and whip with cream and butter. Season with nutmeg and salt to taste. Place in a casserole and brown under broiler. Place pheasants on hot serving dish. Garnish with warmed ham strips; surround with sauerkraut and sausages. Serve with mashed potatoes and pan gravy.

Serves: 4

Wine: Gewurztraminer

Hostellerie du Cerf

Marlenheim, France

Chef: Robert Husser

FAISAN A LA VIGNERONNE

(Pheasant with Grapes)

 1 **young pheasant**
¼ **cup thinly sliced pork fat**
½ **cup white seedless grapes**
½ **cup seeded, halved, red grapes**
¼ **cup butter**
 2 **tablespoons pâté de foie gras**
¼ **cup finely minced shallots**
 4 **slices white bread**
¾ **cup dry white wine**
½ **cup venison stock or beef broth**
 6 **tablespoons heavy cream**
    Salt and freshly ground pepper to taste
½ **cup dry champagne**

Carefully draw the pheasant and lard with pork fat. Reserve liver. Roast bird in a tightly covered Dutch oven for 30 to 35 minutes. During this time, sauté grapes and pheasant liver gently in butter. Reserve grapes and mash liver with foie gras and shallots. Trim and cut bread to make eight triangles; toast. Spread with liver mixture.

When bird is done, remove it to a serving platter and keep warm. Deglaze pan with wine. Add stock and cream and check seasonings. To serve, disjoint pheasant and slice breast. Arrange sautéed grapes and toast triangles around the bird and coat the pheasant with sauce. Flame with champagne and serve at once while very hot. This dish is traditionally accompanied by choucroute (sauerkraut) and spaetzles (egg dumplings).

Serves: 2

Wine: Pommard

Welcombe Hotel

Stratford-upon-Avon, England

Chef: J. M. Vallade

CAILLES AUX RAISINS

(Quail with Grapes)

 8 **quail**
 2 **tablespoons sweet butter**
½ **cup dry white wine**
 1 **tablespoon Curaçao**
¼ **cup white grape juice**
 2 **tablespoons concentrated beef broth**
    Salt and freshly ground pepper to taste
 1 **cup green grapes**

Rub quail with butter and roast in a moderate (350° F.) oven for about 45 minutes, basting every 8 or 10 minutes. When cooked, remove from pan to a warmed serving platter. Pour wine, grape juice and Curaçao into the pan in which quail were roasted. Boil rapidly, scraping up juices, to reduce to about ¼ cup. Add beef broth and simmer for 2 or 3 minutes. Check seasoning. Pour over quail and decorate with grapes.

Serves: 4

Wine: Loire Sancerre, Château de Sancerre

Tiberio

London, England

Chef: Leoni Cristiani

QUAGLIETTE DI VIGNA A LA BACCHUS

(Quail with Polenta)

4 quail
¼ teaspoon garlic powder
3 tablespoons parsley butter
  Salt and freshly ground pepper to taste
1 tablespoon lard
1 cup polenta (cornmeal)
½ cup butter

Rub inside of quail with garlic, parsley butter, salt and pepper. Coat outside with lard. Roast in a moderately hot (375° F.) oven for about 45 minutes, basting every 10 minutes.

While quail are roasting, bring 5 cups heavily salted water to a rolling boil. Gradually pour in the cornmeal, stirring constantly and not losing the boil. Cook slowly for ½ hour, stirring constantly with a wooden spoon. This will be very thick when done. Remove the polenta and place it in a buttered dish in a 1-inch-thick layer.

Cut out four slices of polenta and sauté in butter until lightly brown. Place on serving dish with a quail on each. Garnish with a dollop of butter and serve immediately with Insalata Cesare (see index).

Serves: 2

Wine: **Gattinara di Spanna**

Capion

Millau, France

Chef: Edmond Capion

GRIVE DE CAUSSES AU FOIE D'OIE

(Thrush with Goose Liver)

1 thrush
¼ cup fresh pork fat
½ cup goose liver
¼ cup chopped black truffles
½ teaspoon grated nutmeg
½ cup Madeira
  Potato chips

Bone the thrush entirely without cutting through the skin of the bird; then wrap it in pork fat. Place it in a very hot (450° F.) oven for about 15 minutes. Stuff it with the goose liver and black truffles, sprinkle lightly with nutmeg and return it to the oven for 5 minutes. Deglaze pan with Madeira. Serve the thrush in a nest of potato chips; pour pan liquid over bird as sauce.

Serves: 2

Wine: **Marcilly Première 1964**

Dubern

Bordeaux, France

Chef: Robert Dibar

LA BECASSINE, AINSI QUE FAISAIT MON PERE

(Snipe the Way My Father Prepared It)

1 1½-pound (750-gram) snipe, woodcock or Cornish hen
3 slices pork fat
3 tablespoons cognac
1 cup game stock, made with giblets, trimmings and carcass
1 tablespoon flour
½ cup foie gras
   Salt and freshly ground white pepper to taste
½ teaspoon ground nutmeg
2 slices fried white bread
3 tablespoons cognac
1 tablespoon butter

Hang snipe for several days in a dry, cool place. (In this way it will obtain an incomparable flavor.) Remove the intestines. With a trussing needle take out the gizzard (above the hip). Truss the bird and roast it covered with the sliced pork fat. Take the bird out when the pricked breast gives off a pink drop.

Cut the snipe into quarters, adding the carcass to the stock. Skim the fat from the pan juices. Ignite the pieces of snipe with 3 tablespoons of cognac.

Thicken game stock with flour and deglaze roasting pan with it. Add foie gras, salt, white pepper and nutmeg. Knead the mixture. Spread foie gras mixture on fried bread slices. Put them in a chafing dish to finish cooking. Ignite bread with the remaining cognac. When the flame is out, arrange snipe on bread and add butter to the pan. Heat gently until juice is very thick. Pour pan juice over all.

Serves: 2

Wine: Pomerol

Les Provencaux

Brussels, Belgium

Chef: M. F. Meyrath

PIGEONNEAUX EN ETOUFFADE

(Young Pigeons Braised in a Casserole)

2 squab pigeons
½ cup butter
4 slices ham
½ cup sliced mushrooms
½ cup chopped onions
½ cup cognac
3 tablespoons concentrated veal broth

Wash and thoroughly dry the pigeons. Melt butter in a deep flameproof casserole. Brown birds on all sides over medium heat, being careful not to burn. When birds are brown, remove from casserole. Brown ham slices and set aside. Let pan cool a minute or two; then add mushrooms and onion and sauté until onion is limp. Remove vegetables and set aside. Deglaze pan with cognac. Add veal broth. Return pigeons, ham, mushrooms and onions to casserole. Cover tightly and cook in a moderately slow (325° F.) oven for about 45 minutes. Serve hot.

Serves: 2

Wine: Château Lescour

Ristorante Savini
Milan, Italy
Chef: Sante Guerini

FAGIANELLA ALLA SAVINI

(Moor Hens Savini)

- 2 moor hens (fagianella) or small chickens
- 2 thick slices bacon
- ½ cup butter
- 1 tablespoon olive oil
- ½ teaspoon rosemary
- ¼ cup juniper berries
- ¼ cup finely chopped onion
- ½ cup dry white wine
- ¼ cup cognac
- ½ cup diced carrots
- 1 cup peeled, diced potatoes
- ½ cup sliced artichoke hearts
- ½ cup sliced mushrooms
- ½ cup peas
- ¼ cup pitted black olives
  Butter

Clean moor hens inside and out thoroughly. Tie slices of bacon onto breasts. Put hens in an uncovered pan with butter, olive oil, rosemary, juniper berries and onion, and place in a moderate (350° F.) oven. Baste often. When the birds have browned, spoon the wine and cognac over them and return to oven until completely cooked. This should take about 1 hour.

Meanwhile, combine carrots, potatoes, artichoke hearts, mushrooms, peas and olives; sauté in a pan with butter.

Serve the fagianella on a hot dish accompanied by the mixed vegetables.

Serves: 6

Wine: Barolo Barbaresco

Le Canadian Club
Brussels, Belgium
Chef: M. Paul Grauwels

PINTADEAU AUX RAISINS DE MUSCAT

(Guinea Chick with Raisins)

- 1 1½-pound (750-gram) guinea chick or Cornish hen
- ½ cup cognac
- 1 cup white muscat raisins, plumped in ¼ cup boiling water
- ½ cup white muscatel wine
- 1 teaspoon white vinegar
  Salt and freshly ground pepper to taste
- 2 tablespoons butter

Cook guinea chick in a shallow uncovered casserole in a moderate (350° F.) oven until very tender. When well done, drain pan juices from casserole and discard. Flame chick with cognac. Remove chick and keep warm. Put into the casserole with the liquid in which the raisins were soaked, the white muscatel wine and the white vinegar. Bring to a boil and reduce by a third. Season to taste. Pour raisins into sauce; do not boil. Before serving, add butter.

Halve chick and pour sauce over. Serve with potato croquettes, if desired.

Serves: 2

Wine: Château Bel Air 1959

Section Four

DUCKS AND GEESE

Parc des Eaux-Vives
Geneva, Switzerland
Chef: Ido Viale

POTTED DUCK WITH LIVER PATE

¼ **cup finely chopped lean pork**
¼ **cup finely chopped green bacon**
¼ **cup finely chopped duck meat**
2 **tablespoons cognac**
2 **tablespoons Madeira**
   Salt to taste
1 **tablespoon coarsely chopped truffle**
¼ **cup fresh goose liver**
   Pastry (recipe follows)

Mix pork, bacon and duck with cognac, Madeira, water to cover meat and salt. Let stand in a cool place for 24 hours; then drain and mix meats thoroughly. Add truffle to pâté mixture. Leave goose liver in one piece. Place pâté mixture in a springform mold with goose liver in center. Set to chill while Pastry is being made.

Pastry

1 **cup flour**
1 **teaspoon salt**
½ **cup lard**
1 **egg**

Sift flour and salt together. Cut in lard until mixture resembles coarse cornmeal. Beat egg and add to dough, mixing thoroughly. Add ¼ cup cold water, a tablespoon at a time, just until a stiff dough forms. Wrap pastry in waxed paper and chill for at least 3 hours.

Conclusion

1 **egg yolk**
1 **cup lard (optional)**

Roll out dough to ¼-inch thickness. Gently unmold chilled pâté onto pastry. Wrap and shape dough to completely enclose pâté. Seal seams with a little water. Carefully transfer pâté to a baking sheet (a very large spatula or another cookie sheet used as a spatula helps in this operation). When the enclosed pâté is resting right-side up (seam-side down) on the baking sheet, brush pastry with egg yolk beaten with 1 tablespoon water and cut 2 good-sized slits in top so that steam can escape as the pâté bakes.

Bake in a moderately hot (375° F.) oven for about 45 minutes, or until the pastry is completely done and nicely browned. Let stand out of oven for 20 minutes. Pâté can then be served as a hot first course or side dish or cooled to room temperature.

As pâté cools, it will shrink somewhat. When it is thoroughly cool, melted lard may be poured into pastry jacket through the steam vents to completely seal the meat. Preserved in this way, the pâté will keep for a month in a cool place.

Serves: 2 to 4

Parc des Eaux-Vives

Geneva, Switzerland

Chef: Ido Viale

CANARD AU CITRON

(Lemon Duck)

   2 **pounds (1 kilogram) meaty veal bones**
   2 **lemons**
   ½ **cup sugar**
   1 **4-pound (2-kilogram) duck, with giblets**
   1 **cup dry white wine**
   ½ **cup Noilly Prat**
   1 **tablespoon cornstarch**
   1 **egg**
   ½ **cup buttered bread crumbs**
   1 **lemon, thinly sliced**

Make 2 cups stock from the veal bones and meat. Peel lemons, reserving peels, and cook in 1 cup water with sugar. When lemons are tender, press through a sieve to squeeze all juice from pulp. Reserve lemon syrup mixture. Cook the lemon peels in water until tender. Set aside.

Roast duck and giblets; it should be still rare. Add ½ cup white wine to the duck pan juices and meat from veal bones. Reduce by half and reserve.

Put lemon-syrup mixture, the remaining white wine and the Noilly Prat into a saucepan. Reduce by half. Thicken veal stock slightly with cornstarch and add. Cook for 15 minutes; then add reserved concentrated duck sauce.

Slice breast meat of duck and keep warm. Separate thighs and legs and dip them first in egg beaten with 2 tablespoons of cold water and then in bread crumbs. Bake in a very hot (450° F.) oven for about 20 minutes, or until very tender and crisp.

To serve, arrange sliced breast and legs on a platter. Pour sauce over breast slices (serve extra sauce separately) and garnish all with lemon slices.

Serves: 4

Wine: Vosne-Romanée or Morey St. Denis

Le Petit Bedon
Paris, France
Chef: Jacques Tiéc

La Maison du Cygne
Brussels, Belgium
Chef: M. Van Gasbecq

FOIE DE CANARD AUX POMMES
(Duck Liver with Fried Apples)

     3 or 4 duck livers, depending on size
   ½ lemon
     Salt and freshly ground pepper to taste
     3 tablespoons flour
     Butter
1¼ cups pared, cored and sliced tart apples
     1 tablespoon sugar
   ¼ cup butter
   ½ cup port
   ½ cup veal stock
   ¼ cup butter

Rub livers with lemon. Dust with salt and pepper and dredge in flour. Brown livers in a little butter in a heavy skillet. Place in a moderate (350° F.) oven for 10 to 15 minutes, depending on size of livers. Meanwhile, sprinkle apples with sugar and sauté in ¼ cup butter. Set aside.

When livers are fork-tender, place them on a serving dish. Pour off fat left in the skillet and deglaze with port. Reduce sauce mixture by two-thirds and add veal stock. Cook for 10 minutes. Taste for seasonings and beat ¼ cup butter into sauce.

Arrange fried apple slices around livers and reheat gently in oven. Coat the livers with the hot sauce and pass extra sauce.

Serves: 2

CANETON AU POIVRE VERT
(Duckling with Green Pepper)

   1 2-pound (1-kilogram) duckling
 ¾ cup cooked rice
 ¾ cup ground veal
 ¼ cup diced green pepper
 ¼ cup heavy cream
 ¼ cup butter
     Salt and freshly ground pepper to taste
 ½ cup chopped onions
 ½ cup dry white wine
   1 tablespoon beef stock
 ½ cup cognac
     Freshly ground pepper to taste
   1 cup pea purée

Wash and dry duckling. Make stuffing with rice, veal, green pepper, 1 teaspoon cream, 1 teaspoon butter, salt and pepper. Stuff the duckling and put in a hot (400° F.) oven for 45 to 50 minutes. Just before it is finally cooked, skim off fat. Add 1 teaspoon butter and chopped onion to the pan. Remove duck and keep warm. Reduce pan juices by half; add wine, 2 teaspoons heavy cream and beef stock. Reduce by half again. Adjust seasoning to taste; add cognac, pepper, remaining butter, softened, and remaining cream. Pour cream sauce over duckling and serve with pea purée.

Serves: 2

Casina Valadier

Rome, Italy

Chef: Bertoldti Voltaire

ANATRA ALL'ARANCIA

(Duck with Orange Sauce)

    1 5-pound (2.5-kilogram) duck
    2 tablespoons butter
    1 carrot, sliced
    1 stalk celery, diced
    ¾ cup Grand Marnier
    ½ cup Madeira
    ¾ cup cognac
       Juice of 2 oranges
       Juice of 1 lemon
    ¼ cup cranberry sauce
    2 cups chicken consommé
    1 orange peel, cut in thin strips
    1 lemon peel, cut in thin strips
    ¼ cup sugar
    3 tablespoons vinegar

Roast duck in a moderate (350° F.) oven for 10 minutes. Add butter, vegetables and neck of the duck, and cook for 1 hour. Pour Grand Marnier over duck and flame it. Add Madeira, cognac, orange and lemon juice, cranberry sauce and chicken consommé, and cook for a further 15 minutes in a slow (250° F.) oven. When duck is done, remove from roasting pan and keep warm.

Strain pan liquid and reduce to 1 cup. Blanch the orange and lemon peel. Drain. Finish the sauce by boiling together the pan juices, 2 tablespoons water, sugar, vinegar and blanched orange and lemon peel. Pour sauce over the duck and serve immediately.

Serves: 6

Wine: Barolo Opera Pia

Copenhagen
Paris, France
Chef: E. Pedersen

LE CANARD SALE A LA DANOISE

(Salted Duck Danish-Style)

  1 4½-pound (2.25-kilogram) duck
  4 cups coarse salt
1¼ cups sugar
  5 tablespoons saltpeter
     Bouquet Garni (see index)
  4 cups fish stock
 ½ cup diced potatoes, cooked
 ½ cup diced carrots, cooked
 ½ cup diced turnips, cooked
 ½ cup fresh spinach, cooked
 ½ cup cut asparagus, cooked
 ¼ cup melted butter

Marinate duck in 12 cups water mixed with salt, sugar, saltpeter and Bouquet Garni for four to five days.

Remove duck and poach it in fish stock for 1 hour and 45 minutes. When done, the flesh of the duck should be pink, the color of pickled pork.

Serve with boiled potatoes, carrots, turnips, spinach and asparagus, all dressed with melted butter.

Serves: 4

Wine: Bieus Aquant

Europejski
Warsaw, Poland

DUCK WITH APPLES

  3 tablespoons salt
  2 5-pound (2.5-kilogram) ducks
 ½ teaspoon powdered marjoram
 ½ cup melted pork fat
 ¼ cup melted butter
  6 apples
 ¼ cup sugar
  1 tablespoon salt
 ⅛ teaspoon marjoram

Thoroughly salt the ducks and rub the insides with powdered marjoram. Put in very hot (450° F.) oven and baste with the melted fat and butter. When ducks are turning golden, baste with ½ cup of water and reduce the temperature slightly. Roast until tender, basting from time to time with pan liquid. When done the ducks should be brown and crisp. Set aside and keep warm.

Peel the apples, cut in quarters and core. Keep in slightly acid water (add a dash of vinegar or lemon juice) until ready to cook. Then put apples into an enamel saucepan; add 3 tablespoons of fat from the roasting pan, sugar, salt and marjoram. Stew, covered, until apples are tender. Serve apples with each serving of duck.

Serves: 10

Wine: Dry red wine

Lucas Carton
Paris, France
Chef: Comey

CANARD ROUENNAIS A LA ROUENNAISE

(Pressed Duck)

1 4-pound (2-kilogram) duck, strangled
2 cups Bourgogne
1 lemon peel
1 orange peel
  Cognac
¼ cup fresh goose liver
2 teaspoons brown prepared mustard
1 teaspoon dry white wine
¼ cup butter
1 teaspoon salt
  Freshly ground pepper to taste
¾ cup Bordelaise sauce*

Draw the duck, reserving liver and lungs, and roast it in a very hot (450° F.) oven for 20 minutes. While duck roasts, boil down by half the Bourgogne wine with lemon and orange peels. Add cognac and ignite. Simmer duck liver and lungs and goose liver until tender in a little salted water. Mash liver and lungs through a fine sieve. Reserve.

Prepare the mustard by thinning it with white wine. Mix with a fork the goose liver, butter, salt, pepper and the liver and lungs.

Cut up the duck. Separate legs and thighs; slice breast. Rub legs and thighs with mustard mixture and broil. Cut up the carcass and press to get blood and juices. Place the breast fillets on a serving dish and keep warm.

Heat Bordelaise sauce over a low flame. Add to it the boiled-down Bourgogne and then the goose liver mixture. To this (fairly thick) sauce, add the duck blood and juices. Stir well with a wire whisk. Pour sauce over breast slices. Serve thighs and legs afterward.

Pressed duck is traditionally served with soufflé potatoes (or potato chips) and Duxelles (see index).

Serves: 2

*Prepared Bordelaise sauce may be used in this recipe, or it can be made from 1 cup brown sauce, ¼ cup white Bordeaux wine, 2 tablespoons each of finely minced onion and mushroom and a sliver of garlic, all simmered together for 30 minutes.

Wine: Bourgogne

Rôtisserie de la Reine Pédauque
Paris, France
Chef: M. Soubirou

CANETON NANTAIS A L'ORANGE

(Duckling with Orange Sauce)

- 1 5½-pound (2.75-kilogram) dressed duckling, with trimmings and giblets
- 2 small onions
- 2 carrots
- 1 teaspoon oil
- 3 cups jus brun (meat stock)
  Bouquet Garni (see index)
- 4 navel oranges
  Salt and freshly ground pepper to taste
- 3 tablespoons sugar
- ¼ cup wine vinegar
- 2 tablespoons arrowroot
- 1 tablespoon lemon juice
- 2½ tablespoons Curacao

Chop up the trimmings and giblets, onions and carrots. Brown them in oil in a saucepan. Pour off the oil, add the meat stock, Bouquet Garni and a little water. Simmer for 1½ hours, skimming occasionally. Strain.

Peel the oranges and blanch peels in boiling water for 15 minutes. Drain and cut into fine slivers. Season the inside of the duckling with salt and pepper; add one-third of the orange peel and truss. Prick the skin around the legs and lower breast. Brown in a hot (425° F.) oven for 15 minutes; then lower the heat to moderate (350° F.), turning the duck on one side for 30 minutes and the other side for 20 minutes. Return to an upright position and roast for 15 minutes more.

Meanwhile prepare the sauce. Boil the sugar and vinegar over a medium flame until it becomes a dark syrup. Remove from heat and pour in one-quarter of prepared stock. Simmer a few minutes, stirring until the syrup is dissolved. Mix the arrowroot with lemon juice and Curacao; add the remaining stock and the arrowroot mixture to the hot sauce. Stir in orange peel and heat through. Place duck on a heated platter and keep hot. Skim all fat from the roasting juices and boil remaining juices to reduce to about 3 tablespoons. Pour over the duckling. Serve sauce separately.

Serves: 4

Wine: Aloxe-Corton 1964

Tour Eiffel
Paris, France
Chef: Robert Saget

DUCKLING "BELLE EPOQUE"

  1 5-pound (2.5-kilogram) duckling
    Salt and freshly ground pepper to taste
  2 onions, finely chopped
  2 carrots, finely chopped
  2 leeks, finely chopped
  3 tablespoons butter
  ½ cup dry white wine
  4 cups veal gravy
    Thyme
  1 bay leaf
  2 tablespoons cornstarch
  5 dozen pitted sour cherries
  ¼ cup kirsch
  ¼ cup sugar
  ¼ cup vinegar
  ¼ cup Grand Marnier

Season the duckling with salt and pepper. Roast in a very hot (450° F.) oven or cook on spit but not until dry.

Sauté vegetables in butter. Moisten with wine and veal gravy. Add thyme and bay leaf. Cook for about 2 hours. Strain and thicken with cornstarch.

Soak cherries in kirsch. Boil down sugar and vinegar to a caramel. Add to gravy and wine mixture. Stir in cherries and Grand Marnier. Heat through.

To serve, set duckling in deep dish and pour on sauce. Serve very hot.

Serves: 4

Wine: Bordeaux rouge, Château Lynch Bages 1964 Pauillac

Chez Puget (Le Petit Brouant)
Nice, France
Chef: Gaston Puget

CANARD BEAULIEU

(Duck with Artichokes)

  2 3-pound (1.5-kilogram) ducks
    Salt and freshly ground pepper to taste
  3 tablespoons butter
  ½ cup dry white wine
    Roux (optional)
  2 artichokes
 12 small new potatoes
  2 tomatoes, peeled, seeded and chopped
    Pitted black olives

Prepare stock with necks, wings, giblets and 3 cups water. Simmer 30 minutes. Draw and truss the ducks. Season with salt and pepper and rub lightly with butter. Roast in a moderate (350° F.) oven for about 30 minutes. Baste well during cooking. When ducks are done, remove to a serving platter and keep warm.

Deglaze pan with wine; add stock and continue cooking until reduced by one-half. Skim off all fat. Thicken with roux, if desired. Taste for seasonings.

Simmer artichokes in water to cover for 30 to 45 minutes, or until leaves are easily removed. Boil new potatoes. To serve, arrange quarters of the artichokes and whole potatoes around ducks. Decorate platter with chopped tomatoes and olives. Pass sauce separately.

Serves: 4

Wine: Blanc che Bellit

Le Berlioz
Paris, France
Chef: Jean Claude Musseau

CANETON A L'ORANGE
(Duckling with Orange Sauce)

½ cup sugar
6 tablespoons vinegar
3 oranges, peeled and sliced
4 cups white meat stock
¼ cup flour or cornstarch
  Salt
  Cayenne
1 4½-pound (2.25-kilogram) duckling
2 tablespoons larding fat
2 oranges, 1 quartered, 1 sliced
  Salt and freshly ground pepper to taste
1 orange peel, blanched

Prepare light caramel sauce by cooking sugar, vinegar and orange slices until sugar melts and turns golden. Deglaze pan with white meat stock. Reduce by two-thirds. Strain sauce and blend it with flour or cornstarch. Season with salt and cayenne. Continue cooking for 30 minutes.

Draw duckling, and fry in the fat in a skillet. When the duckling is cooked, placed it on a serving plate and decorate it with slices and quarters of orange. Skim all the fat off the skillet, pour in the sauce and let cook for a few minutes. Check the seasonings, strain the sauce and add blanched orange peel. Pour sauce over the duckling and serve immediately.

Serves: 4

Wine: Château Houit Marbuzet

Domaine de la Tortinière
Montbazon, France
Chef: G. Mazeau

CANARD AUX CERISES
(Duck with Cherries)

2 4-pound (2-kilogram) ducks
1 tablespoon cherry liqueur
2 cups white meat stock
1 cup sugar
½ cup wine vinegar
1 cup pitted sweet cherries, well drained

Roast the ducks till medium done, or about 40 minutes in a hot (400° F.) oven. Cut out fillets, deglaze the pan with cherry liqueur, add white meat stock and let boil down until reduced by half. Strain and reserve.

Cook sugar with wine vinegar to obtain a light caramel. Mix into the caramel the sauce from the duck pan. Let mixture boil 10 minutes.

Arrange the fillets on heatproof plate and add the cherries. Cover with the sauce and put into the oven to heat through.

Serves: 4

Wine: Chinon Rouge 1969

Lapérouse
Paris, France
Chef: Fernand Poisson

CANETON DE COLETTE

(Duckling "Colette")

- 1 5-pound (2.5-kilogram) duckling
- ½ cup veal stock
  Salt and freshly ground pepper to taste
- ¼ teaspoon fines herbes
- ¼ teaspoon sweet basil
- ¼ cup brandy
- ¼ cup port
- 2 tablespoons butter

Draw the duck; flame it to burn off pin feathers and clean the outside. Remove the wishbone to facilitate carving. Roast the duck for 25 minutes; flesh should be pink. Meanwhile simmer duck liver in veal stock (two livers might be needed); leave them rare, crush with a fork and add the salt and pepper, the spices, the brandy and the port. Ignite and let liquid reduce during flaming.

Slice the duck breast and arrange on an oval platter. Remove the duck thighs. They should be very rare. Cook in butter in a tightly covered pan until very tender.

Cut the carcass in half and squeeze it in order to obtain the maximum quantity of blood and juice. Stir these into the reducing liver liquid. Bring sauce to a boil, check the seasoning and strain through a fine sieve onto the breast slices and thighs of the duck.

Serves: 3

Wine: Côte-Rôtie la Grosse Roche 1959

54

Lamazère
Paris, France
Chef: Henri Ricottier

LE VERITABLE CASSOULET LAMAZERE AU CONFIT D'OIE

(Casserole of White Beans and Preserved Goose)

- 1 pound (500 grams) dry white beans
  Salt and freshly ground pepper to taste
- 1 teaspoon fines herbes
- ½ cup chopped onions
- 1 clove garlic, minced
- ½ cup chopped carrots
- ¼ pound (120 grams) pork rind, thinly sliced
- 1 pound confit d'oie* or leftover roast goose
- 1 pound Toulouse sausage† or mild pork sausage
- 1 pound (500 grams) salt pork, diced
- 1 pound (500 grams) ham, diced
- 1 tomato, peeled and chopped

Soak the beans in cold water overnight. Heat to boiling. Discard this water and cover the beans with fresh cold water, adding salt, pepper, fines herbes, onion, garlic, carrots and the pork rind slices.

When beans are almost cooked, add confit d'oie, Toulouse sausage, pork, ham and tomato. Cook very slowly for 3 or 4 hours. When the gravy becomes smooth and creamy, pour the cassoulet into an earthenware dish and bake in a very slow (200° F.) oven until gravy is brown.

Serves: 6

*Goose pieces preserved in goose fat in earthenware pot.
†Sausage made of hand-minced pork and kept for at least six weeks with goose fat in a stoneware container.

Wine: Cahors or red Bordeaux

Section Five

CHICKEN

Pagoda
Madrid, Spain
Chef: Chien Soi Shien

CHICKEN MANDARIN

1 2¼-pound (1-kilogram) spring chicken, cut in pieces
2 small bamboo shoots
1 stalk spring onion
2 tablespoons Chinese mushrooms, soaked as directed on package
¼ cup oil
2 tablespoons Chinese wine
6 tablespoons dark soy sauce
1 cup chicken stock or water
1 tablespoon sugar
Dash of monosodium glutamate
½ teaspoon cornstarch, mixed with a little cold water

Wash chicken in cold water. Cut bamboo shoots into small pieces and shred spring onion and mushrooms. Heat oil in pan and sauté onion for a few minutes. Place chicken in pan, add bamboo shoots and mushrooms and continue frying. When chicken changes color, add wine, soy sauce and sufficient stock or water to cover chicken. Cook for 20 minutes. Add sugar and simmer for 30 minutes. Finally, add monosodium glutamate. Thicken sauce with cornstarch-and-water mixture and serve hot.

Serves: 4

Speilen, A/S Grand Hotel
Oslo, Norway
Chef: Nicolo Castracaner

CHICKEN BREAST BOHEMIENNE

12 chicken breasts
½ cup butter
Salt and freshly ground pepper to taste
¾ cup sherry
1 tablespoon paprika
15 tarragon leaves, chopped
2¼ cups heavy cream
½ cup fresh pimientos, cut in squares
1 cup mushrooms, sautéed
2 cups rice pilaf
1 teaspoon arrowroot

Remove all bones from chicken breasts and gently sauté in butter with salt, pepper and sherry until lightly browned. Add paprika, tarragon and cream. Cook for about 15 minutes.

Arrange breasts in a silver dish; decorate with pimientos; trim with sautéed mushrooms and rice pilaf. Thicken the sauce remaining in the pan with arrowroot. Pour some of this over the meat and put the remainder in a sauceboat.

Serves: 6

Rôtisserie des Cordeliers

Nancy, France

Chef: M. Antoine

URSULINE DE NANCY

(Chicken Dumplings)

1 3-pound (1.5-kilogram) chicken
  Eggs (see below)
  Salt and freshly ground pepper to taste
2 tablespoons chopped truffles
1 cup heavy cream
½ cup sliced raw mushrooms
¼ cup butter
¼ cup chopped shallots
¼ clove garlic
  Salt and freshly ground pepper to taste
  Puff pastry
½ cup pâté de foie gras
1 cup Périgueux sauce [Madeira Sauce (see index) with chopped truffle]
1 cup buttered asparagus tips

Bone chicken entirely; reserve bones, trimmings and giblets. Grind the meat and measure it. For each ½ cup, blend in one egg. Refrigerate mixture for 24 hours.

The next day: Place meat in mixing bowl and add salt and pepper. Add chopped truffles and check seasoning. Thin meat mixture with enough cream to make a soft, thick dough.

Prepare 1 cup white meat stock from chicken bones and trimmings in which to poach the puréed mixture. Form purée into finger-shaped dumplings and simmer in stock until firm. Drain and keep warm. Sauté mushrooms in butter with shallots and garlic. When soft, blend them with remaining cream and let boil down. Season with salt and pepper. Cut prepared puff pastry into five rectangles about 5 inches by 3 inches. Bake without filling.

To serve, place mushrooms in the center of each puff pastry; top with pâté de foie gras and finally chicken dumplings. Pour Périgueux sauce all over and decorate with buttered asparagus tips.

Serves: 10

Wine: Chambolle Musigny Amouresse 1964

Nandron

Lyon, France

Chef: ID

POULET SAUTE AU VINAIGRE

(Sautéed Chicken with Vinegar)

1 3½-pound (1.75-kilogram) chicken, cut in pieces
  Salt and freshly ground pepper to taste
½ cup butter
6 tablespoons tarragon vinegar
6 tablespoons dry white wine
1½ cups crushed fresh tomatoes

Season chicken pieces with salt and pepper and brown in 2 tablespoons butter. When the chicken is golden brown, deglaze skillet with tarragon vinegar and white wine. Add crushed fresh tomatoes and let simmer. When chicken is done, remove the pieces and reduce the sauce by half; then strain through a fine sieve. Beat the rest of the butter into sauce. Check seasoning. Pour the sauce over the chicken and serve with rice, if desired.

Serves: 4

Wine: Beaujolais Morgon

Hotel de L'Abbaye
Talloires, France
Chef: Pierre Marchand

POULARDE DE BRESSE FARCIE AUX ECREVISSES

(Stuffed Bresse Chicken with Crayfish)

2 2-pound (1-kilogram) Bresse* chickens
½ cup ground rump of veal
2 tablespoons heavy cream
  Salt and freshly ground pepper to taste
2 pounds (1 kilogram) crayfish
  Butter
1 teaspoon flour
2 tablespoons cognac
¼ cup butter
¼ cup heavy cream
¼ cup béchamel sauce
2 tablespoons cognac
4 thin slices pork fat
1 cup Mirepoix (see index)
2 tablespoons cognac
2 tablespoons butter, melted
  Watercress sprigs

Bone and skin one of the chickens. Chop the meat finely and mix with ground veal. Beat meats into the cream. Add salt and pepper.

Sauté crayfish in butter until shells are red. Reserve four whole crayfish for garnish. Shell tails and reserve the meat. Crush shells through a fine sieve and mix with butter remaining in skillet and flour to thicken. Stir into chicken-veal-cream mixture 2 tablespoons of the shell sauce (Nantua). Flame crayfish tails with cognac and add to stuffing.

Pulverize crayfish bodies. Stir in ¼ cup butter, ¼ cup cream and béchamel sauce. Add any shell sauce left from preparation of stuffing. Strain through cheesecloth and check seasonings. Reserve.

Rinse and pat the second chicken dry. Ignite with cognac and fill the cavity with stuffing. Truss and lard chicken with pork fat. Place it in a deep pot with a tight lid. Add to pot mirepoix and trimmings and carcass of the first chicken. Bake in a slow (250° F.) oven until chicken is very tender, about 1 hour. When chicken is done, remove to a warm serving platter and deglaze pot with cognac. Strain liquid from the pot through a fine sieve and add to sauce.

To serve, place reserved whole crayfish around the chicken and spoon melted butter over chicken. Decorate platter with sprigs of watercress. Serve sauce from a sauceboat.

Serves: 4 or 5

*A town in France known for its fine chickens.

Wine: Santenay or Volnay

Les 3 Dômes, Hotel Sofitel

Lyon, France

Chef: Marc Alix

JAMBONNETTES DE VOLAILLE LUCULLUS

(Stuffed Boned Chicken)

   1 1½-pound (750-gram) chicken
   ½ cup Madeira
   6 tablespoons heavy cream
   1 egg yolk
      Salt and freshly ground pepper to taste
  10 cockscombs, sliced
  10 poultry livers, sliced
   ½ cup foie gras, sliced
   1 truffle, minced

Bone the chicken, splitting the back and leaving on the neck skin, as it will serve to make the jambonnettes with the wings. Leave a piece of the drumstick bone and of the wingtips on the chicken—these will be used for making the cuffs. Place boned chicken flat on a plate and cut into quarters carefully so that the skin covers each quarter well. Remove one slice of meat from each breast and reserve for stuffing. Save any small trimmings.

Prepare the stuffing from slices of breast and any extra flesh. Press out the fat from the thighs. Chop meat and fat very thoroughly and blend with 2 tablespoons Madeira, cream, egg yolk, salt and pepper. Add a mixture of cockscombs, poultry livers, foie gras and truffle. Stuff each quarter of chicken and sew the skin to form pig-knucklelike shapes (jambonnettes).

Cook the jambonnettes in a lightly buttered pan, covered, for 25 minutes on a low flame to avoid bursting. Deglaze pan with remaining Madeira and cover again to finish cooking, basting from time to time.

Serves: 2

Wine: Château Pichon-Lalande 1962

Le Nord

Lyon, France

Chef: Claude Ovise

POULET SAUTE A L'ESTRAGON

(Chicken Sauté Tarragon)

   1 3-pound (1.5-kilogram) chicken, cut in pieces
   ½ cup butter
   2 cups rich veal stock
   ¼ cup fresh tarragon sprigs
   ¾ cup heavy cream

Brown chicken pieces in butter; then remove excess fat from pan. Over the meat pour veal stock and add fresh tarragon sprigs tied together. Cook, covered, until chicken is fork-tender, about 30 minutes. Remove chicken pieces and keep warm. Discard tarragon bouquet. Finish the sauce by adding cream and a little more chopped fresh tarragon, if desired. Correct seasonings and cover the chicken parts with the sauce. Serve with rice, if desired.

Serves: 4 or 5

Wine: Bourgogne or Beaujolais

Le Vert Galant

Paris, France

Chef: Garnier

LA POULARDE DE BRESSE AU POT HENRI IV

(Bresse Chicken in the Pot)

¼ **pound pork fat**
1 **chicken liver**
¼ **cup chopped shallots**
¼ **cup chopped parsley**
1 **clove garlic**
2 **eggs**
½ **cup soft bread crumbs**
1 **4½-pound (2.25-kilogram) chicken**
    Bouquet Garni*
1 **pound (500 grams) pork breast**
3 **large carrots, halved**
2 **medium turnips, halved**
1 **medium green cabbage, quartered**

Chop first five ingredients finely, or run through a food mill. Mix thoroughly with eggs and bread crumbs.

Stuff the chicken with this mixture and truss it. Place chicken and Bouquet Garni in a casserole with a lid and cover with water. Bring to a boil and simmer gently until chicken is very tender, about 1¾ hours.

Cook pork breast for 15 minutes in salted water to cover; then add carrots, turnips and cabbage. Cook over a high flame for 50 minutes, then for another 10 minutes over a low flame, or until vegetables are tender and pork is done.

Cut the chicken into quarters and the pork into slices. Serve in soup plates with the vegetables and the bouillon arranged around meats.

Serves: 4

*Parsley leaves, celery stalk, a leek, thyme and a bay leaf secured with string for easy removal.

The Empress

London, England

Chef: G. Scandolo

COQ AU VIN

(Chicken with Wine)

1 **4-pound (2-kilogram) young chicken**
½ **cup butter**
¼ **pound (120 grams) larding bacon, diced**
1 **cup sliced mushrooms**
1 **cup tiny onions**
    Salt and freshly ground pepper to taste
    Bouquet Garni (see index)
1 **clove garlic**
½ **cup brandy**
1½ **cups dry red wine**
½ **cup chicken livers, sieved**

Cut chicken into quarters and sauté it in butter together with bacon, mushrooms, onions, salt and pepper. When golden add Bouquet Garni and garlic and flame with brandy. Add red wine and simmer until tender. The sauce can then be thickened with sieved chicken liver. Do not allow to boil. Correct seasoning and serve with croutons fried in butter, if desired.

Serves: 4

Wine: Romanée St. Vivant, Les Quatre Journaux, Louis Latour 1962

F. Point, La Pyramide

Vienne, France

Chef: Guy Thivard

POULARDE DE BRESSE PYRAMIDE
(Truffled Chicken)

¼ cup sliced truffles
1 3- to 6-pound (1.5- to 3-kilogram) roasting
   chicken, trussed
   Butter
½ cup sliced carrots
½ cup sliced leeks
¼ cup diced celery
2 cups white meat stock
½ cup dry white wine
   Salt and freshly ground pepper to taste
   Sauce (recipe follows)

Slip slices of truffles through small slits in the breast skin of the roasting chicken. Brown chicken on all sides in a little butter in a heavy pan with a tight cover. When golden, remove chicken and place carrots, leeks and celery in the bottom of the pot to form a bed for braising. Return chicken to pot and add white meat stock and wine. Season with salt and pepper and cover tightly. Simmer gently on top of the stove or in a slow (250° F.) oven until chicken is very tender, about 1½ hours. Turn the chicken from time to time. Add more meat stock during braising if necessary.

To serve, place chicken on a serving dish. Mix Sauce into strained cooking liquid. Arrange vegetables around the chicken and spoon sauce over both. Pass extra sauce.

Sauce

¼ cup flour
¼ cup butter
½ cup chicken broth
2 whole cloves
1 small onion
¼ cup finely diced carrots
2 or 3 egg yolks, beaten
   Salt and freshly ground pepper to taste

In the top of a double boiler over very hot water, cook flour in butter for about 5 minutes, stirring constantly. Add broth and mix well. Insert cloves in onion and add to sauce. Mix in finely diced carrot. Thicken the sauce with egg yolks. Season with salt and pepper.

Serves: 4 to 6

Wine: Côte-Rôtie

Bingley Arms
Bardsey, Leeds, England
Chefs: Ian Walker and Christopher Haw

CHICKEN BINGLEY ARMS

1 3½-pound (1.75-kilogram) chicken
2 or 3 thin slices smoked lean bacon
¼ cup self-rising flour
  Pinch salt
1 tablespoon wine vinegar
  Freshly ground pepper to taste
¼ teaspoon marjoram
¼ teaspoon thyme
¼ teaspoon chopped parsley
½ cup oil
½ cup dry white wine
½ cup heavy cream
2 sprigs parsley
1 cup sweet corn kernels

Remove breasts from chicken; skin and cut off wings leaving 1-inch of wing bone clear of meat. Wrap breasts in bacon slices. Set aside.

In a large mixing bowl, combine flour, salt, vinegar and ½ cup water. Mix to the consistency of thick cream. Season with pepper, marjoram, thyme and parsley. Let stand for 30 minutes. A little of the liquid will have risen to the top. Beat thoroughly to reestablish creamlike consistency. Dip chicken in this batter, holding it by the wing bone to ensure that the coating is uniform. Heat oil in an electric skillet and add chicken. Fry slowly at 300° F. until chicken is brown—about 5 to 7 minutes. Remove chicken to a heatproof serving dish and place in a moderate (350° F.) oven for 5 minutes. This allows excess cooking oil to drain and the batter to become crisp enough to take the sauce without becoming soft.

While chicken is in the oven, prepare a sauce using the white wine and cream. Pour sauce over chicken, avoiding the wing bone. Place cutlet frill over bone and garnish with parsley sprigs. Serve immediately with sweet corn.

Serves: 2

Hyde Park Hotel
London, England
Chef: Pierre Beaufort

POITRINE DE POULET CLUNYSOISE
(Chicken with Champagne Sauce)

1 cup butter
1 cup flour
7½ cups chicken stock
2 cups dry champagne
1¼ cups heavy cream
1 3-pound (1.5-kilogram) chicken
½ cup rice, cooked
¼ cup sautéed chicken livers
¼ cup butter
Salt to taste
6 chicken breasts
½ cup button mushrooms, sautéed
½ cup veal quenelles, cooked
24 asparagus spears, boiled

Melt butter in large saucepan and make a roux with the flour. Bring chicken stock to a boil and blend well with roux. Reduce heat and simmer for 2 hours, or until the sauce becomes smooth and thick. In a separate saucepan reduce the champagne by half. Add to velouté and blend well. Warm cream and add; simmer until sauce is thick and creamy. Check for seasoning.

While the sauce is cooking, fill the chicken with rice and liver. Truss the chicken and rub with butter and salt. Place in a casserole and bake for 1 hour and 10 minutes in a moderate (350° F.) oven. Baste with cooking juices every 10 or 15 minutes. Add chicken breasts to casserole, basting with the juices, and bake for 20 minutes more. Remove chicken and breasts from casserole and place on a serving dish. Garnish with mushrooms and quenelles. Pour strained sauce over chicken and breasts. Decorate with asparagus spears.

Serves: 6

Wine: Bourgogne Aligot 1966

WHEELER'S SOVEREIGN
London, England
Chef: Man Ying Sau
Sole Pommery
(page 122)

THE RUSSELL
Dublin, Ireland
Chef: Jackie Needham
Saumon Froid en Belle Vue
(page 144)

NORMANDIE RESTAURANT
Birtle, near Bury, England
Chef: J. P. Champeau
Homard "Champeau"
(page 162)

Charles Barrier
Tours, France
Chef: Charles Barrier

FRICASSEE DE POULARDE CARDINAL LA BALUE

(Chicken with Crayfish Sauce)

1 2½-pound (1.25-kilogram) chicken
  Salt and freshly ground pepper to taste
  Butter
1 dozen crayfish
1 cup fish stock
1 cup butter
3 cups heavy cream

Cut the chicken into eight pieces. Season lightly with salt and pepper and fry in butter until light brown. Continue cooking in a moderate (350° F.) oven, uncovered, for about 45 minutes, or until fork-tender. In the meantime, boil the crayfish 5 minutes in the fish stock. Shell tails and reserve them. Crush shells, strain through a fine sieve and mix the purée with butter. When chicken is done, arrange pieces in a casserole (place thighs and wings on bottom, tender breast pieces on top) and cover. Keep warm.

Deglaze the chicken skillet with cream; reduce by half. When ready to serve, place crayfish tails and crayfish purée on top of chicken. Check seasonings in sauce and pour over chicken and crayfish. Heat through and serve immediately very hot.

Serves: 4

Wine: Chinon or Bourgueil

London Hilton
London, England
Chef: Oswald Mair

POUSSIN SAUTE AU MOUTON CADET

(Baby Chickens with Red Wine Sauce)

8 ¾-pound (375-gram) poussins (baby chickens)
6 tablespoons butter
2 tablespoons brandy
2 cups chicken stock
1 cup red Mouton Cadet
  Salt and freshly ground pepper to taste
½ cup heavy cream
¼ cup cèpes*
¼ cup morels
½ cup small white mushrooms
2 tablespoons goose liver pâté

Cut poussins in quarters, heat butter in sauté pan and lightly brown chicken pieces. Flame with brandy, add stock, wine and seasoning. Cover the pan and braise in moderate (350° F.) oven until tender. This should take about 20 minutes. Remove chicken and keep warm in earthenware dish.

Reduce stock, add half the cream, cèpes, morels and white mushrooms and simmer until sauce thickens slightly. Finally, add pâté and the remainder of the cream. Adjust seasoning to taste and pour over poussin portions.

Serves: 8

*A flat mushroom. If not available, increase white mushrooms to ¾ cup.

Wine: Mouton Cadet red

Ivy Restaurant
London, England
Chef: Leon

FRICASSEE OF CHICKEN IVY

7½ cups mussels in shells, scrubbed
 ¼ cup sliced onion
     Salt and freshly ground pepper to taste
 2 tablespoons oil
 1 cup butter
 4 chicken breasts
     Salt and freshly ground pepper to taste
 ½ cup button mushrooms
 1 cup small onions, boiled
     Thyme
 1 bay leaf
 6 white peppercorns
 ¼ cup flour
 ½ cup dry white wine
 5 tablespoons heavy cream
     Juice of 1 lemon

Steam mussels in 2 cups water, onion, salt and pepper until shells are open. Remove mussels from cooking liquid and set both aside.

Heat oil and butter in a heavy saucepan. Season chicken breasts with salt and pepper and sauté them for about 15 minutes. They will be a very light golden color. Do not brown. Add mushrooms, half the boiled onions, thyme, bay leaf and peppercorns. Cover and simmer for 20 minutes. Remove the breasts, mushrooms, onions and herbs and set aside.

Add flour to the same pan and make a roux. Add wine and sufficient mussel stock to make a creamy velouté. Simmer for 10 minutes, or until sauce thickens. Check seasoning. Strain sauce into a fresh pan and add the chicken breasts, mushrooms and onions to the sauce. Simmer gently for 15 minutes. Add cream and shelled mussels. Check seasoning. Squeeze lemon juice over all and stir in. Serve with rice pilaf, if desired.

Serves: 4

Wine: Château Bellevue St. Emilion 1964

Mumtaz
London, England
Chef: Addul Noor

PUNJABI CHICKEN

1 3-pound (1.5-kilogram) chicken, quartered
2 tablespoons oil
1 cup finely chopped onions
  Salt to taste
1 inch fresh gingerroot, chopped
4 or 5 cloves of garlic, chopped
6 green cardamoms
6 black cardamoms
2 cinnamon sticks
3 or 4 bay leaves
1 teaspoon turmeric
¼ cup tomato purée
½ teaspoon chili powder (optional)
6 tablespoons sugar
¼ cup white vinegar
  Juice of 1 lemon
½ cup heavy cream

Remove skin from chicken. Heat oil in large skillet and lightly sauté onions. Add salt, gingerroot and garlic. Stir. Add cardamoms in their shells, cinnamon sticks and bay leaves. Cook over low heat until onions are browned, stirring occasionally. Add chicken and turmeric. Cover and simmer over low heat about 20 minutes. Add tomato purée and chili powder. Simmer and stir for 5 minutes.

Mix sugar, vinegar and lemon juice. Add to chicken. Increase heat and continue stirring vigorously until sugar begins to burn and onion to turn dark brown. Stir in cream and cook for another 2 or 3 minutes. Serve with rice, pilaf or any Oriental bread, if desired.

Serves: 6

Grand Hotel Margitsziget
Budapest, Hungary
Chef: Bálint Miklós

GODOLLO STUFFED CHICKEN

3 2-pound (1-kilogram) chickens
3 slices lean back bacon
6 tablespoons lard
1 goose liver, cut into small cubes
6 tablespoons sliced mushrooms
¼ cup soft butter
2 eggs
1 teaspoon tomato purée
3 slices stale bread, soaked in warm water and squeezed dry
2 sprigs parsley, finely chopped
1½ teaspoons salt
  Pinch freshly ground black pepper
  Pinch marjoram

Wash chicken in cold water and dry thoroughly. Cut bacon into small cubes and fry lightly in lard. Add goose liver and mushrooms and fry. Beat butter well with eggs; add tomato purée, bread, parsley, salt, pepper and marjoram. Combine with fried goose liver and mushrooms. Knead this mixture well and stuff chickens with it. Truss chickens and roast in a moderately slow (325° F.) oven for 1½ hours, or until birds are golden and juice running from a pricked thigh is clear instead of pink.

Serve with potato chips or steamed rice, if desired.

Serves: 8

Wine: Chablis

Grosvenor House

London, England

Chef: Roger Couchie

SUPREME OF CHICKEN, LA FONTAINE

>   2 whole breasts of chicken with wings attached
>   1 whole chicken leg
> 1½ cups heavy cream
>   5 tablespoons medium-dry sherry
>   2 teaspoons salt
>   4 slices pâté de foie gras
>   2 tablespoons flour
>   2 tablespoons salad (not olive) oil
>   1 pound (500 grams) white potatoes
>   1 cup butter
>   Salt and freshly ground pepper to taste
>   2 egg yolks
>   16 3-inch asparagus tips, cooked
>   8 artichoke hearts, cooked
>   2 medium tomatoes, peeled, seeded and chopped
>   ¼ cup finely chopped shallots
>   Salt to taste
>   8 Fluted Mushrooms (see index)
>   ½ cup sliced mushrooms
>   ¼ cup brandy
>   ½ cup port
>   Truffle slices

Remove first and second joints of wings, leaving only first wing bones attached to breasts. Split breasts down the center to make four suprêmes. Remove and discard breast bones. Take meat from detached joints of chicken wings and whole leg; mince it very fine in a food mill. To the chicken meat, add ½ cup cream, 1 tablespoon sherry and 2 teaspoons salt.

Place suprêmes on a board and make a pocket in the center of each piece about 3 or 4 inches long, taking care not to cut through the meat underneath. Pipe chicken mousse mixture into slit and place a slice of pâté de foie gras on top of mousse inside slit. Lightly flour stuffed suprêmes on both sides and sauté gently, slit side down, in oil for 10 to 15 minutes. Turn suprêmes to cook on the other side.

Meanwhile peel and dice potatoes. Cook until very tender in boiling water just to cover. Drain potatoes and add ¼ cup butter. Shake pan over heat to melt butter and dry out cooked potatoes. Season with salt and pepper and mash into a purée. Add egg yolks and beat potatoes until mixture is thick and fluffy. Pipe potatoes onto a greased cookie sheet in four rectangular cups about 4 inches by 2 inches. Bake in a moderate (350° F.) oven a few minutes until potatoes no longer stick to the sheet. Grill under broiler to brown slightly. Keep warm.

Gently heat asparagus tips and artichoke hearts separately in 2 tablespoons butter each in small pans. Sauté chopped tomatoes, shallots and salt in 2 tablespoons butter until most of the tomato liquid has evaporated and mixture is thick. Place four asparagus tips in each potato cup and 2 tablespoons of the tomato mixture in each artichoke heart. Keep warm. Sauté Fluted Mushrooms in 2 tablespoons butter and reserve.

Sauté sliced mushrooms in ¼ cup butter; add brandy, port and the rest of the sherry, cream and tomato mixture. Adjust seasonings.

Place suprêmes on a large serving platter. Decorate with truffle slices and Fluted Mushrooms. Arrange potato cups and artichoke hearts around chicken, pour sauce over suprêmes and serve at once.

Serves: 4

Wine: Corton-Charlemagne white or Mouton Cadet red

Fem Små Hus

Stockholm, Sweden

CHICKEN ACAPULCO

1 ¾-pound (375-gram) chicken
  Salt and freshly ground pepper to taste
¼ cup olive oil
1¾ cups diced mango
1 tablespoon lemon juice
2 tablespoons cornstarch
2 slices orange, peeled
2 slices pineapple

Cut chicken into four pieces; remove backbone and discard or save for stock. Season chicken with salt and pepper and fry in olive oil in a casserole until golden brown. Meanwhile, force mango through a sieve and mix with lemon juice. Pour the resulting purée over browned chicken, add about ¼ cup water and stir. Allow to simmer, covered, for about 10 minutes, or until chicken is done.

Mix cornstarch with ¼ cup cold water and stir into the casserole. Bring to boil.

Garnish with slices of orange and pineapple. Serve with rice and lettuce, if desired.

Serves: 2

Terrazza
London, England
Chef: Carlo Avogadri

PETTO DI POLLO VESUVIO

(Chicken Breast with Eggplant)

    1 medium eggplant
    1 tablespoon salt
   ¼ cup flour
    1 egg, beaten
   ¼ cup butter
    1 whole breast of a roasting chicken
   ¼ cup flour
    1 egg, beaten
   ¼ cup white bread crumbs
    2 tablespoons butter
    2 tablespoons oil
    2 cups peeled, seeded and chopped fresh plum
      tomatoes
   ¼ cup olive oil
    1 clove garlic, crushed
    1 teaspoon dried sweet basil
      Salt and freshly ground pepper to taste
    2 slices mozzarella cheese
    2 sweet basil leaves
    2 tablespoons melted butter

Peel and halve eggplant, salt it and leave for 1 hour between two heavy plates. Afterwards, squeeze halves dry, dip in flour and beaten egg and sauté in butter.

Bone, skin and split breast. Slightly flatten the pieces. Dip them in flour, then in beaten egg and finally in bread crumbs. Sauté breasts in butter and oil until tender. Meanwhile, cook tomatoes, oil and herbs together very slowly until tomatoes disintegrate and sauce is thick and smooth, about 2 hours. Stir often to prevent scorching. Season with salt and pepper.

Season chicken to taste and place on serving dish. Over each piece pour a little of the tomato sauce, then top with an eggplant half. Cover eggplant with some more tomato sauce. Over this, place a slice of mozzarella and top with a leaf of sweet basil. Pour a little melted butter over all and place in a moderate (350° F.) oven for 5 minutes before serving.

Serves: 2

Wine: Bolla Bardolino

La Napoule

London, England

Chef: Giulio Imperato

SUPREME DE VOLAILLE LA NAPOULE

(Chicken Breast with Foie Gras)

- 1 whole chicken breast with wings attached
- 6 tablespoons pâté de foie gras
- 1 sprig tarragon, finely chopped
  Butter
  Salt and freshly ground pepper to taste
- 1 julienne carrot
- 1 julienne leek
- ¼ cup chopped mushrooms
- 1 teaspoon finely grated lemon peel
- 1 tablespoon whiskey
- ¼ cup dry white wine
- ¼ cup heavy cream
- 2 tablespoons butter
  Duchesse Potatoes (see index)
- 8 large Fluted Mushrooms*
- 1 teaspoon meat glaze

Split breast down the middle. Remove and discard breast bone and tips of wings. Leave wing bone attached to breast. (The breast-and-wing combinations are the "suprêmes.") Make a slit in the breasts and stuff suprêmes with pâté de foie gras. Season with tarragon, and sauté in melted butter to seal meat. Season with salt and pepper. Add carrot, leek, chopped mushrooms and lemon peel to the pan containing the suprêmes. Sauté gently. When carrot is cooked, add whiskey and flame; then add white wine. Reduce cooking liquid by half and finish by adding cream and butter.

Pipe a serving dish with Duchesse Potatoes and let color under grill. Decorate with sautéed Fluted Mushrooms. Place suprêmes in the dish, cover with sauce and decorate with meat glaze.

Serves: 2

*Flute mushrooms by holding them in one hand and with the other cutting a series of consecutive slits in the caps, radiating out from the centers to the edges.

Wine: Chassagne-Montrachet 1966 (Bouchard Ainé)

Criterium

Antwerp, Belgium

Chef: Van de Eynde Constant

POULARDE POINCARE

(Chicken with Lobster)

1 2½-pound (1.25-kilogram) pullet
  Salt and freshly ground white pepper to taste
2 cups dry white wine
2 shallots, chopped
1 bay leaf
1 tablespoon salt
8 crayfish
1 small lobster or 1 cup cooked lobster meat
2 tablespoons butter
4 fresh truffles
8 cockscombs or thin slices parboiled sweetbreads, sautéed
8 cock kidneys or thin slices lamb kidneys, sautéed
1 cup Waleska Sauce (recipe follows)
1 cup Mornay Sauce (see index)

Wash and dry bird. Season inside and out with salt and white pepper. Truss. Roast in a moderately slow (325° F.) oven until very tender, about 1½ hours.

While pullet roasts, bring wine, 2 cups water, shallots, bay leaf and salt to a boil and cook the shellfish in the mixture until shells are red. Remove from stock (reserve stock for sauce). Keep crayfish warm. When lobster is cool enough to handle, remove meat from shell and cut in large pieces. Melt butter in a small pan and add lobster meat. Toss just to heat through and coat with butter. Set aside and keep warm.

When pullet is done, put it on a deep serving platter. Place crayfish and truffles around bird and arrange cockscombs and kidneys on top of it. Pour Waleska Sauce around the pullet and garnish platter with buttered lobster meat and potato croquettes, if desired. Spoon Mornay Sauce over all.

Waleska Sauce

  Reserved shellfish stock
½ teaspoon powdered thyme
½ teaspoon fines herbes or 1 teaspoon minced fresh green herbs
½ cup heavy cream
2 tablespoons butter

Reduce stock to 1 cup. Strain; discard shallots and bay leaf. Add thyme and herbs. Simmer 10 minutes. Remove from heat. Add cream, stirring constantly, and cook until sauce is thickened. Do not let boil after cream is added. Finally, add butter in small pieces, beating until all butter is incorporated and sauce is creamy. Check seasonings. Keep warm.

Serves: 4

The Russell

Dublin, Ireland

Chef: Jackie Needham

CHICKEN CHAUD-FROID

2 3½-pound (1.75-kilogram) chickens

2 carrots, sliced

2 onions

2 whole cloves

½ tablespoon salt

2 cups heavy cream

1 cup butter

1 cup flour

  Salt and freshly ground pepper to taste

2 tablespoons unflavored gelatin

2 cups chicken consommé

2 tomatoes, sliced

½ cup pitted black olives, sliced

½ cup chopped leeks (green portion)

Truss chickens and cook for 35 minutes in water to cover with carrots, onions (with a clove inserted in each) and salt. When chickens are cooked, remove from water and allow to cool. Cover chickens with a damp cloth.

Reduce chicken stock by half. Strain stock and add cream. Reduce still further and thicken with a roux of butter and flour. Remove from heat and add salt and pepper to taste. Soften the gelatin in ¼ cup cold water. Add half of it to the sauce. Chill.

Bring consommé to a boil. Add other half of softened gelatin. Chill until aspic is the consistency of unbeaten egg whites.

Quarter each chicken and remove skin. When cold, cover with sauce and allow to set. Decorate chicken portions with tomato slices, olive slices and leeks. Finally, coat chicken with aspic jelly. Arrange on silver dish and decorate with chopped aspic jelly.

Serves: 4 to 6

Wine: Château la Faite

Hotel Maria Thérèsia
Innsbruck, Austria
Chef: M. Erich Mair

SUPREME DE VOLAILLE HOTEL MARIA THERESIA

(Chicken Breast with Risotto)

    1 2-pound (1-kilogram) chicken
      Salt to taste
    ¼ cup chopped carrots
    ¼ cup chopped celery
    ¼ cup chopped leek
      Peppercorns
      Risotto (recipe follows)
      Cream Sauce (recipe follows)

Quarter the chicken and boil it in 3 cups lightly salted water with carrot, celery, leek and a few peppercorns till tender. Lift fowl out of the stock; skin and bone it. Keep breasts warm in some of the stock. Dice the rest of the chicken for risotto.

Risotto

    1 tablespoon chopped onion
    ¼ cup sliced mushrooms
    1½ tablespoons olive oil
    ½ cup rice
    1 cup chicken stock
    2 tablespoons dry white wine
    1½ tablespoons grated Parmesan cheese
    1 tablespoon butter
    1 cup raw green peas
    1½ tablespoons butter

Sauté onion and mushrooms in oil until light brown. Add rice and cook and stir until rice is light tan. Add all other ingredients except the 1½ tablespoons butter and cook, tightly covered, until all liquid is absorbed. Add butter and reserved diced chicken. Check seasonings.

Cream Sauce

    1½ tablespoons butter
    ¼ cup flour
    1 cup chicken stock
    1 egg yolk
    2 tablespoons heavy cream
    1 teaspoon lemon juice
      Salt
      Pinch nutmeg

Melt butter in top of double boiler over hot, not boiling, water. Add flour, stir briskly and work to a light-colored paste. Pour in chicken stock and cook for 10 minutes, stirring constantly. To complete the sauce, add egg yolk, cream, lemon juice, salt and nutmeg.

Conclusion

    ½ cup finely shredded cooked beef tongue
    2 truffles, sliced

Mound risotto on a round heatproof serving platter. Split chicken breasts and arrange on top. Sprinkle with shredded tongue. Pour sauce over chicken and risotto. Garnish with sliced truffles. Place the platter in a very hot oven just until the surface of the sauce glazes and barely begins to brown.

Serves: 4

Wine: Riesling Auslese, Winzergen, Wachau-Durnstein

Lafayette
Dublin, Ireland
Chef: Roger Noblet

SUPREME DE VOLAILLE MARCEL
(Chicken Breasts in Pastry Shells)

    1 breast of a 4-pound (2-kilogram) chicken
    ¼ cup pâté de foie gras
      Caul fat or unsalted bacon strips
    2 tablespoons butter
    ½ cup sherry or dry white wine
    ½ cup heavy cream
      Salt and freshly ground pepper to taste
    2 tablespoons butter
    ½ cup sliced mushrooms
      Juice of 1 lemon quarter
    1 tablespoon flour (optional)
    1 tablespoon butter (optional)
    2 cups puff pastry

Bone the full breast of chicken and skin it. Open out by slicing down center. Spread foie gras inside. Fold closed, making sure foie gras is sealed inside meat. Wrap in caul fat or bacon and sauté slowly in 2 tablespoons butter (omit butter if bacon is used) for 20 minutes. Fat should be white.

Remove breast and take off caul fat; keep chicken warm. Drain off cooking butter, allowing sediment to remain in pan. Add sherry or white wine and cream; bring to boil, then reduce heat. Adjust seasoning and add 2 tablespoons butter; strain.

Place mushrooms in a saucepan; add lemon juice and half the cream sauce. Bring to boil; simmer for 10 minutes. Thicken with a roux of flour and butter if necessary.

Shape puff pastry into two individual tart cases and bake. Remove when golden.

To serve, put creamed mushrooms into each puff-pastry case, place one-half of the breast of chicken on top and coat with reserved cream sauce.

Serves: 2

Wine: Riesling 1967

Gourmet
Milan, Italy
Chef: Gigi Pontiroli

"CRESPELLE" GOURMET
(Chicken-Mushroom Crêpes)

    ⅔ cup flour
    1 cup milk
    4 eggs, beaten
    1 tablespoon minced parsley
    ½ teaspoon nutmeg
    1 cup cooked, diced chicken
    ½ cup mushrooms, minced
    4 small pieces truffle, minced
    ½ cup béchamel sauce (white sauce made with milk)
    ¼ cup grated Parmesan cheese

Mix flour with milk, adding eggs, parsley and nutmeg. With this mixture, prepare twelve thin crêpes ("crespelle"); place them on a cloth and let cool. Combine chicken, mushrooms and truffle, spread on the pancakes and roll them up. Place in a gratin dish, cover with béchamel sauce and sprinkle with cheese. Put the crespelles under the broiler until sauce and cheese are golden brown.

Serves: 4

Wine: Bolla Bertani Bardolino 1966 or 1967

Section Six

MEATS

Restaurant Napoléon

Paris, France

Chef: Guy Baumann

BIFTEK TARTARE MARECHAL DUROC

(Tartar Steak)

⅔ cup finely ground top grade beef
1 egg yolk
1 tablespoon minced parsley
1 teaspoon minced chives
1 teaspoon minced chervil
1 teaspoon minced tarragon
1 pickled gherkin, chopped
1 tablespoon capers
¼ peeled tart apple, chopped
   Salt and freshly ground pepper to taste
½ teaspoon steak sauce or Worcestershire sauce
½ teaspoon catsup (optional)

Mix all ingredients thoroughly but gently. Shape in the form of a steak on serving plate. Chill thoroughly before serving.

Serves: 4 as hors d'oeuvres
or 1 as main course

Hotel Pension Schwarzenberg

Vienna, Austria

ROASTED FILLET OF BEEF IN CREAM SAUCE

1 3-pound (1.5-kilogram) fillet of beef
½ cup lard
   Salt and freshly ground pepper to taste
1 cup chopped carrots
1 cup chopped parsley root
1 cup chopped celery
1 cup sour cream

Prepare fillet of beef by trimming away fat, membranes and the thin end; spread the meat with the lard and season with salt and pepper. Roast the fillet with vegetables in a hot (400° F.) oven for 18 to 20 minutes. Separate the meat from the juice and vegetables; strain the juice, discard vegetables and boil juice. Add sour cream to the hot juice, but do not reboil. Serve the meat in slices covered with the cream sauce. Serve remaining sauce separately.

Serves: 4 or 5

The Barrie Grill
Kensington Palace Hotel
London, England
Chef: Larry Stove

FILLET OF BEEF WELLINGTON

    1 4-pound (2-kilogram) fillet of beef
    4 pounds (2 kilograms) mushrooms, sliced
    ½ cup butter
    1 cup white sauce
    1 cup brown sauce
    2 tablespoons white wine
    ¾ cup Madeira
    2 pounds prepared puff pastry
    1 small truffle, sliced

Partially roast the beef (approximately 15 minutes). Allow to cool while you sauté the mushrooms in butter, adding the white and brown sauces, the white wine and the Madeira. Coat the beef with this mixture. Roll out the pastry and wrap it around the beef fillet. Top with sliced truffle and cook in moderately slow (325° F.) oven for 30 minutes.

Serves: 6 to 8

Malta Hilton

Malta

FALDA
(Stuffed Brisket)

    1   5-pound (2.5-kilogram) beef brisket
    2½ pounds (1.25 kilograms) minced beef
    4   eggs
    ½   cup chopped onions
    2   sprigs parsley, chopped
        Salt and freshly ground pepper to taste
    4   cups beef stock

Slit brisket to form a pocket. Combine remaining ingredients except the beef stock. Stuff the brisket with this mixture. Sew the gap up so that it is completely sealed. Boil in beef stock for about 1½ hours, or until meat is very tender. Remove meat from liquid and serve sliced either hot or cold.

Serves: 10

Malta Hilton

Malta

LUCERTO
(Beef with Potatoes and Onions)

1 4-pound (2-kilogram) silverside of beef
1 cup thickly sliced carrots
1 clove garlic, slivered
8 cups thickly sliced potatoes
4 cups sliced onions
5 cups beef stock
  Salt and freshly ground pepper to taste
2 tablespoons lard
5 sprigs parsley, chopped

Cut small incisions into the fat side of the beef and tightly press in slices of carrot and slivers of garlic. Boil in the stock for approximately 20 minutes.

Prepare a casserole dish with layers of sliced potatoes and sliced onions. Add remaining garlic. Place meat on top; moisten with stock; add lard and cook in a moderate (350° F.) oven for about 30 minutes, or until very tender.

Serve accompanied by the onions and potatoes garnished with parsley. Strain the stock and serve separately.

Serves: 10

Jadran

Dubrovnik, Yugoslavia

Chef: Stijepo Turanjanin

DALMATINSKA PRZOLICA
(Beef Fillet with Beet Greens)

3¼ cups beet greens
 ½ cup olive oil
  2 tablespoons crushed garlic
2½ cups potatoes
  1 1¾-pound (875-gram) fillet of beef, cut into 5 pieces

Wash beet greens thoroughly and shake off excess water. Do not dry. Place in covered saucepan with 3 tablespoons oil and ½ tablespoon garlic. Steam over very low heat until tender, about 20 minutes. Boil the potatoes in a separate saucepan at the same time. When vegetables are nearly done, rub the beef fillets with oil and grill (or broil) to desired doneness. Arrange beef on serving platter surrounded by potatoes and beet greens. Sprinkle the remaining oil and garlic over the meat.

Serves: 5

Wine: Plavac

Esplanade Intercontinental

Zagreb, Yugoslavia

Chef: Martin Maček

DALMATIAN PASTITSADA

(Beef Dalmatian-Style)

  7 tablespoons salt

  1 4½-pound (2.25-kilogram) fillet of beef

10 strips smoked bacon

  1 cup salad oil

  1 cup sliced onions

  1 cup sliced carrots

  1 cup sliced celery

     Pinch garlic powder

     Pinch cinnamon

  1 bay leaf

  8 cups beef broth

  7 tablespoons flour

  1 cup tomato purée

  2 cups dry red wine

  7 tablespoons chopped pitted prunes

  7 tablespoons lemon juice

  1 tablespoon black pepper

Rub salt into the meat thoroughly and secure bacon strips around the beef. Heat ½ cup oil in a large skillet and brown meat thoroughly on all sides. Remove meat to large flameproof serving dish. Set aside. In the browning oil (add more if necessary), sauté onion, carrots and celery until soft. Stir in garlic, cinnamon and bay leaf. Pour vegetables and their cooking oil over the beef, add 6 cups beef broth and simmer until tender, about 45 minutes. Remove beef and set aside, keeping it warm.

Make a roux with flour and remaining oil and add to cooking liquid, stirring constantly over low heat until thoroughly blended. Sauce will begin to thicken. Add tomato purée, wine, prunes, lemon juice, pepper and remaining beef broth. Bring to a boil and stir constantly until mixture is quite thick. Put sauce through a sieve. Pour over the beef and serve immediately. Serve with potato dumplings or boiled bread rolls (a dumpling-like specialty), if desired.

Serves: 10

Wine: Red Burgundy

Restaurant Excelsior
Amsterdam, Netherlands
Chef: J. Dresscher

TOURNEDOS EXCELSIOR

   Salt and freshly ground pepper to taste
1 ½-pound (250-gram) fillet of beef
1 tablespoon butter
¼ cup minced onion
¼ cup minced leeks
1 tablespoon whiskey or cognac
¼ cup dry red wine
¼ cup sliced mushrooms
¼ cup sliced smoked ox tongue
1 tablespoon heavy cream
1 teaspoon Worcestershire sauce
   Garlic powder
1 sprig parsley, minced

Season the fillet of beef (tournedos) and sauté on each side with sufficient butter to prevent meat juices from running out. Remove from frying pan. Add onion to the butter and sauté gently. Now add leeks. Return tournedos to frying pan and cook on both sides. Pour in whiskey and flame; then quench with red wine. Remove tournedos and arrange on dish. Add mushrooms to sauce in the frying pan; as mushrooms are cooking, add sliced smoked ox tongue. Continue cooking until sauce has thickened. Add cream, Worcestershire sauce and garlic powder to taste. Pour sauce over tournedos and garnish with fresh minced parsley.

Serves: 1

Hotel International

Brno, Czechoslovakia

GOULASH A LA SVRATKA

1   2-pound (1-kilogram) beef sirloin
⅓   cup diced bacon
½   cup minced onion
2   teaspoons paprika
1   teaspoon flour
¼   teaspoon marjoram
¼   teaspoon chili powder or dried flakes
1½   tablespoons catsup
1½   cups beef stock
     Salt to taste

Slice beef into strips about ½ inch thick. Fry bacon. Add onion and sauté 1 minute. Add beef and brown quickly, approximately 2 minutes. Sprinkle on paprika, flour, marjoram and chili powder and stir thoroughly so that meat is coated. Stir in catsup. Add beef stock and simmer about 10 minutes. Salt to taste. Serve with potato pancakes, if desired.

Serves: 4

Grillroom Spycher
Zermatt, Switzerland
Chef: Max O. Good

FILLET GOULASH A LA SPYCHER

      1 tablespoon butter
      1 sour gherkin, chopped
    ¼ cup minced onion
      1 cup green olives, chopped
    ½ teaspoon crushed garlic
    ¼ cup chopped button mushrooms
      1 canned pimiento, chopped
      2 tablespoons paprika
      1 cup beef stock
    ¼ cup dry white wine
      1 teaspoon salt
    ¼ teaspoon hot pepper sauce
      1 cup sour cream
      1 tablespoon salad oil
    1½ pounds (750 grams) beef tenderloin, cut in
         1-inch cubes

Put butter in a pan with gherkin, onion, olives, garlic and mushrooms and cook for 5 minutes. Add pimiento and paprika and cook for another minute. Add beef stock and wine and cook for another 10 minutes. Add salt, hot pepper sauce and sour cream and heat through. Do not boil after adding cream.

Put oil into another pan and place on high heat until oil is very hot. Brown meat quickly in oil and then place on a hot plate and pour hot sauce over it. Serve with rice and salad, if desired.

Serves: 4

Wine: Red Burgundy

Ristorante "Il Coccodrillo"
Florence, Italy
Chef: Francesco Dei

FILLET OF BEEF, ORLOFF'S-STYLE

      1 tablespoon butter
      2 fresh bay leaves
      1 ½-pound (250-gram) fillet of beef
      2 tablespoons brandy
         Salt and freshly ground pepper to taste
      2 tablespoons cream or milk
    ½ teaspoon French mustard
      5 drops Worcestershire sauce
      5 drops hot pepper sauce
    ½ teaspoon sweet Hungarian paprika
      1 teaspoon minced onion
      1 teaspoon tomato catsup
      2 tablespoons beef gravy
    1½ tablespoons pâté de foie gras (1 slice)

This dish is prepared directly in front of the diner at the table with a spirit lamp. Melt butter in pan and add bay leaves. Place meat in pan and brown it. When the pan is very hot, add the brandy and flame. When the flame has extinguished itself, sprinkle salt and pepper over the meat, then add cream or milk, French mustard, Worcestershire sauce, hot pepper sauce, paprika, onion and catsup. Stir and add gravy. Let simmer, turning fillet now and then until sauce has been reduced and is creamy in texture. This is the moment to place fillet on diner's plate and cover it with the pâté de foie gras. The sauce is then poured over all.

Serves: 1

Wine: Barolo Opera Pia 1958, Brolio Riserva 1964

Hotel International
Varna, Bulgaria
Chef: Stefan Kotarov

STEAK "KOMETA"

1 1¼-pound (620-gram) fillet of beef
  Salt and freshly ground pepper to taste
⅓ cup chopped mushrooms sautéed
¼ cup chopped onion, lightly sautéed
3 egg yolks
2 tablespoons flour
¼ cup vegetable oil
⅓ cup calf brains
1 cup chicken livers
3 tablespoons butter
3 large tomatoes
  Salt and freshly ground pepper to taste
3 slices fried bread
3 tablespoons dry red wine
2 tablespoons butter
2 cups boiled rice
¼ cup cooked green peas
3 sprigs parsley

Cut beef fillet into 3 pieces. Cut a pocket in each piece with a small sharp knife. Salt and pepper meat. In the pocket of each steak put one-third of the mushrooms, one-third of the onion and one raw egg yolk. Close slit in meat with a small skewer. Roll the steak in flour and fry in hot oil. Keep warm.

Soak and parboil calf brains. Cut in ½-inch cubes and sauté with chicken livers in butter. As soon as meats are tender, remove from pan, set aside and keep warm. Plunge tomatoes into boiling water for 1 minute. Cool in cold water and remove skins. Scoop out seeds and pulp. Mince chicken livers; season with salt and pepper. Stuff liver filling into tomatoes.

To serve, remove skewers and place stuffed fillets on slices of warm fried bread. Arrange on serving platter. Spoon sautéed brains over steaks and garnish with tomatoes. Deglaze pan in which beef was fried with wine; add and melt butter. Pour hot sauce over meat. Serve with rice and garnish with green peas and parsley.
Serves: 3

Wine: Red Evksinograd or red Kondov wine

Doney
Florence, Italy
Chef: Alfredo Poggi

TOURNEDOS ANTARES

1 1-pound (500-gram) fillet of beef
1 tablespoon butter
1 cup Marsala
2 slices pineapple
1 teaspoon flour
 Salt and freshly ground pepper to taste
2 round slices fried bread
2 slices pâté de foie gras
2 slices black truffle

Cut fillet of beef into 2 pieces and fry in butter for 6 minutes. When the meat is brown on all sides, add Marsala. Remove fillets and keep hot. Cook pineapple in sauce in pan for 2 minutes, stirring gently. Reduce the pan liquid by half. Thicken with flour mixed with 1 teaspoon cold water. Cook 5 minutes more. Adjust seasonings. Place beef on fried bread on a hot dish. Top with pâté slices and truffle slices and cover with pineapple slices. Pour sauce over all.

Serves: 2

Wine: Villa Antinori 1964

Restaurant Operäkaellaren
Stockholm, Sweden
Chef: Werner Vögeli

BIFTEK AUX HERBES AROMATIQUES

(Steak with Herbs)

1 1½-pound (750-gram) rib eye steak, 2 inches thick, bone in, per person
 Salt and freshly ground pepper to taste
¼ cup chopped shallots
½ clove garlic, pressed
½ cup dry white wine
1 pinch any combination or all of the following herbes aromatiques: chervil, dill, chive, parsley, marjoram, thyme, tarragon
1 tablespoon butter

Season the steak with salt and pepper; then pan broil. Steak must be quite rare. Put on plate and keep warm while making sauce. Add chopped shallots and pressed garlic to the pan. Sauté gently until tender; then add white wine. Allow wine to reduce by half; then add herbes aromatiques. Add butter. Season to taste. Pour over steak and serve with French-fried potatoes and green salad, if desired.

Serves: 1

Wine: Red Burgundy

Gourmet

Milan, Italy

Chef: Gigi Pontiroli

BEEF FILLET "SOUVAROFF"

1 ½-pound (250-gram) tenderloin of beef
2 tablespoons vodka
1 cup concentrated beef stock
½ tablespoon hot mustard
1 tablespoon heavy cream
1 tablespoon butter
1 tablespoon malossol beluga caviar

Put the beef in a very hot (475° F.) oven to roast. When it is browned, remove and flame with vodka. Return to oven and continue roasting until done to taste. Combine stock, mustard, cream and butter. Add caviar. Heat. Spoon sauce over beef and place on a heated dish to serve.

Serves: 1

Wine: Spanna di Gattinara (Vallana) 1958

Grand Hotel

Brno, Czechoslovakia

SIRLOIN A LA GRAND HOTEL

3 pounds (1.5 kilograms) boneless beef sirloin
Salt to taste
¼ pound (120 grams) sliced ham
1 tablespoon oil
¼ cup chopped lean bacon
6 tablespoons chopped onion
Salt and freshly ground pepper to taste
2 tablespoons flour
1 cup beef stock

Rub beef with salt and secure ham slices around beef with string. Heat oil in flameproof casserole dish and fry bacon. Add onion and sauté 1 minute. Add 1 cup water, salt and pepper. Stir in flour thoroughly until well blended; then add beef stock. Bring to a boil and cook for 2 or 3 minutes. Place beef in casserole and simmer, covered, until tender, about 1 hour.

Serves: 6

Old Mill Hotel
Shipston on Stour
Warwickshire, England
Chef: Edward P. Milano

Hotel Budapest
Budapest, Hungary
Chef: István Lukács

FILLET STEAK MILANO

1 fillet steak
2 tablespoons butter
1 tablespoon olive oil
¼ cup finely chopped shallots
½ cup sherry
   Worcestershire sauce
   Fruit sauce
1 tablespoon brandy
1 cup button mushrooms, sliced
¼ cup heavy cream
4 artichoke bottoms, poached
1 teaspoon chopped salsify (oyster plant)

Sauté steak in butter and oil for about 3 minutes on each side for a rare steak, longer for medium rare. Remove, set aside and keep warm. Sauté shallots in the same cooking fat for about 5 minutes. Add sherry, a few dashes of Worcestershire sauce and fruit sauce to taste. Rapidly reduce to a medium-thick consistency—about 1½ teaspoons. Add brandy and mushrooms and cook for 2 minutes, stirring constantly. Remove from heat and stir in cream. Pour over steak. Garnish with artichoke and salsify.

Serves: 1

TENDERLOIN STEAK BUDAPEST

3 slices lean smoked back bacon
⅔ cup lard
½ cup sliced mushrooms
⅔ cup diced goose liver
½ cup chopped green pepper
1 cup concentrated beef stock
1 tablespoon paprika
2 teaspoons salt
5 individual tenderloin steaks (fillets of beef)
3 cups hot cooked rice
¼ cup cooked peas
   Potato chips

Cut the bacon into small cubes; brown evenly in lard. Add mushrooms, goose liver and green pepper, and cook 5 minutes. Add the beef stock and paprika and cook until very thick. Add salt.

    Broil the fillets rare and put them on hot rice on a warm serving plate. Pour the hot sauce over all and sprinkle with green peas. Garnish with potato chips.

Serves: 5

Wine: Beaujolais

Grand Sofia
Sofia, Bulgaria
Chef: Velko Pavlov

BEEF FILLET "VRETENO"

1 1½-pound (750-gram) fillet of beef
   Salt and freshly ground pepper to taste
   Savory
¾ cup sliced mushrooms
1 cup chopped onions
½ cup butter

Cut the fillet into three pieces; cut each one almost through to form a larger, butterfly-shaped piece. Salt, pepper and sprinkle with savory on both sides.

Sauté mushrooms and onion gently in butter. Place filling on butterflied fillets and roll each up like a spindle. Secure with a skewer. Roast on a charcoal grill or broil, turning to brown quickly on all sides.

Serve with pan-fried potatoes and green peas, if desired.

Serves: 3

Wine: Plevenska Gumza

Maison Prunier
London, England
Chef: Jean Lecorre

TOURNEDOS BOSTON

6 shucked oysters, with liquid
1 tournedos
½ tablespoon béchamel sauce
2 tablespoons Hollandaise Sauce (see index)

Poach the oysters in their own liquid just until edges curl. Reduce their poaching liquor to 1 tablespoon; add to it béchamel sauce and Hollandaise Sauce. Grill the tournedos, garnish with the oysters, coat with the sauce.

Serves: 1

Wine: Château Gazin (Pomerol) 1966

Brown's Hotel

London, England

Chef: Peter Morton

LE TOURNEDOS SAUTE ALICE

　　Freshly ground pepper to taste
　8　**6-ounce (180-gram) tournedos**
　½　**cup sweet butter**
　½　**cup shallots**
　¼　**cup fresh tarragon**
　2　**cups Haut-Brion or other Bordeaux**
2½　**cups concentrated beef broth**
　2　**cups tiny onions**
　1　**cup mushroom caps**
　2　**cups asparagus tips**
　16　**small slices foie gras**
　8　**Fluted Mushrooms (see index)**
　1　**bunch watercress**

Generously pepper the tournedos and sauté in ¼ cup butter. Set aside and keep warm.

Chop shallots and tarragon together to make a purée and sauté in the same pan, adding more butter if necessary. Add ¼ cup wine and simmer until dry. Remove mixture to another pan.

Deglaze the first pan with ¼ cup wine and strain onto the tarragon and shallots. Reboil this mixture with concentrated beef broth until a medium-thick sauce is made. To obtain correct consistency, add more wine and the cooking liquid from the braised onions and mushrooms (see below). Melt ¼ cup butter in skillet and sauté the onions and mushrooms. Add 1 cup wine and simmer for about 5 minutes. Remove onions and

mushrooms from cooking liquid. Set aside and keep warm. (Use this reserved liquid in the shallot-tarragon sauce, if necessary.)

Cook asparagus in 2 cups boiling, salted water about 10 minutes, or until done.

Slice tournedos crosswise twice—cutting only three-quarters of the way through. Insert into each slit a slice of foie gras. Place meat on serving platter and arrange mushrooms and onions around it. Cover tournedos with shallot-tarragon sauce and garnish each with a Fluted Mushroom on the top. Decorate with watercress on the side.

Serves: 8

Wine: Romanée-St. Vivant 1959

A l'Ecu de France
London, England
Chef: J. Pedri

CONTRE-FILET DE BOEUF FLAMBE AU VIEUX KIRSCH A LA FAÇON DES TROIS EPIS

(Sirloin of Beef, with Kirsch)

1 6-pound (3-kilogram) sirloin of beef
½ cup Moselle wine
½ cup Vieux Kirsch
4 heads Boston lettuce, braised
2 cups small boiled potatoes, sautéed
¼ cup butter
8 stuffed tomatoes Provençale*

Roast sirloin of beef in hot oven, basting carefully with pan drippings until cooked according to taste. Flavor the gravy with Moselle wine. Immediately before serving, flame sirloin with Vieux Kirsch. Garnish with braised lettuce, sautéed potatoes and tomatoes Provençale.

Serves: 8 to 10

*Stuffed with a mixture of chopped onion, garlic and oregano, sautéed in olive oil and topped with bread crumbs.

Wine: Château Ausone, St. Emilion 1960 or Domaine de Chevalier, Graves 1961

La Ville Lorraine
Brussels, Belgium
Chef: Camille Lurkin

SELLE D'AGNEAU CLOUTEE AUX TRUFFES FRAICHES

(Saddle of Lamb Spiked with Fresh Truffles)

1 3½-pound (1.75-kilogram) trimmed, ready-to-cook saddle of lamb
2 large truffles, cut into strips
½ cup dry red wine
  Salt and freshly ground pepper to taste
8 cooked artichoke hearts
½ cup cooked mashed green beans
2 heads Boston lettuce, braised

Make deep slits with a thin knife in the lamb and insert truffle strips. Roast saddle in a hot (400° F.) oven about 45 minutes. Set meat aside and keep warm.

Deglaze roasting pan with wine and reduce until thick. Season with salt and pepper and pour over meat. Serve with artichoke hearts filled with mashed green beans, braised lettuce and potatoes Anna, if desired.

Serves: 4

Wine: Bordeaux-Médoc

La Napoule

London, England

Chef: Giulio Imperato

CARRE D'AGNEAU EN CROUTE

(Lamb in Pastry)

1 3-pound (1.5-kilogram) sirloin end of a leg of lamb
1 tablespoon seasoned flour
¼ cup butter
¼ cup sherry
1 medium leek, finely chopped
2 small young carrots, finely chopped
½ cup butter
1 teaspoon finely grated lemon peel
4 leaves mint, finely chopped
1 medium slice crustless white bread
¼ cup milk
  Salt and freshly ground pepper to taste
1 cup puff pastry
1 egg yolk
  Périgourdine Sauce (recipe follows)

With a small boning knife, bone the lamb and tie it to retain shape. Sprinkle with seasoned flour. Sauté gently in ¼ cup butter until golden brown. Add sherry and continue cooking for a minute or two; then allow lamb to cool before removing from pan.

To make stuffing, sauté leek and carrots in ½ cup butter together with lemon peel and mint. Soak bread in milk, squeeze to remove excess liquid and crumble into frying pan with vegetables. Season and mix thoroughly.

Roll out puff pastry to form a piece about ⅛ inch thick and large enough to cover lamb. Spread stuffing over pastry to make a bed for the meat. Wrap pastry around the lamb and seal by crimping seams. Decorate with small cutouts of pastry scraps and brush with egg yolk beaten with a tablespoon of cold water. Place in a hot (425° F.) oven and bake for about 25 minutes, or until golden. Serve with Périgourdine Sauce.

Périgourdine Sauce

¼ cup sherry
¼ cup brandy
1 cup veal gravy
¼ cup truffled pâté de foie gras
2 tablespoons butter
  Salt and freshly ground pepper to taste

Combine sherry, brandy, gravy and pâté de foie gras in a saucepan. Bring to a boil. Add butter and stir until it is melted and sauce is smooth. Adjust seasonings. Serve hot.

Serves: 2

Wine: Chambolle-Musigny (Selection of Chevaliers du Tastevin Groffier-Leger)

Quaglino's

London, England

Chef: Peter Ferrero

CARRE D'AGNEAU EN CROUTE
(Crown Roast of Lamb in Pastry)

- 1 **crown roast of lamb**
  Salt and freshly ground pepper to taste
- 1 **pound veal trimmings**
- 2 **boned chicken legs**
- ¼ **cup chopped shallots**
- ½ **cup butter**
- 1 **cup chopped mushrooms**
- ¼ **cup chopped parsley**
- 2 **large black truffles, chopped**
  Salt and freshly ground pepper to taste
- ¼ **cup cream**
- ½ **cup brandy**
- 3 **cups puff pastry**
- 2 **egg yolks**
- 1¼ **cups brown sauce (demiglacé)**
- 18 **cutlet frills**

Season roast and cover exposed ends of rib bones with foil to prevent charring. Roast in a hot (400° F.) oven for 20 to 25 minutes. Remove lamb from oven while it is still slightly pink, remove foil and let lamb cool a little.

Put veal and chicken through mincer. Cook shallots very slowly in 2 tablespoons butter; when tender, add chopped mushrooms and parsley. Let cool and then add minced meat together with 1 chopped truffle, salt, pepper, cream and 2 tablespoons brandy. Spread forcemeat over meat, leaving bones clear.

Roll out puff pastry to ⅛ inch thick. Cover meat and forcemeat with pastry, leaving bone ends bare. Crimp seams and brush with egg yolks beaten with 2 tablespoons water. Put foil back on bones and bake in a hot (425° F.) oven until pastry is done. Remove from oven and let rest for 20 minutes before carving.

Meanwhile heat brown sauce and strain; add other chopped truffle. Finish sauce with the rest of the brandy and butter. Adjust seasoning. Remove foil from bone ends and replace with cutlet frills. Pass sauce separately.

Serves: 6

Wine: Château Clos du Ro, de la Louvières 1966

Asteria Tavern
Athens, Greece
Chef: Athanassios Alexopoulos

MEZELIKIA A LA GRECA

(Lamb Cutlets, Greek-Style)

  2 lamb cutlets, split
  1 veal fillet, cut in small pieces
  ¼ cup poultry liver
  ¼ cup sliced cocktail sausages
  ¼ cup chopped bacon
  ¾ cup oil
  ½ cup butter
    Juice of 1 lemon
    Salt and freshly ground pepper to taste
  1 teaspoon marjoram, preferably wild
    Potatoes Parisienne (see index)

Sauté the meats separately in oil; then place in frying pan and add butter, lemon juice, salt, pepper and marjoram. Cook and stir until flavors are blended. Serve with Potatoes Parisienne. Pour pan juices over all.

Serves: 4

Le Chèvre d'Or
Eze Village, France
Chef: Vincent Barone

GIGOT EN CROUTE EZASQUE

(Stuffed Leg of Lamb in Pastry)

  ½ cup diced carrots
  ½ cup shallots, chopped
  ½ clove garlic
    Butter
  ½ cup bread crumbs
  ½ cup chopped celery stalks with leaves
  ¼ cup chopped mushrooms
  2 eggs
  ¼ cup chopped lean ham
    Salt and freshly ground pepper to taste
  1 whole leg of lamb
  1 cup pork fat
    Pâte feuilletée (flaky pastry)

Cook carrots, shallots and garlic in a little butter until vegetables are wilted and garlic begins to brown. Discard garlic. Mix in bread crumbs, celery, mushrooms, eggs, ham, salt and pepper and blend well.

Bone the leg, leaving the shank bone in. Fill the cavity with the stuffing; tie securely so that leg holds its shape. Arrange fresh pork fat on top of leg and bake in a moderately slow (325° F.) oven for about 18 minutes per pound. When lamb is half baked, stop the cooking and let the meat cool completely. Wrap the cold leg in flaky pastry and finish baking.

Side dishes might include buttered string beans, stuffed tomatoes, oyster plant (salsify) browned in hot fat and pommes Dauphine.

Serves: 6

Le Pavillon de l'Elysée
Paris, France
Chef: Jean Pibourdin

SELLE D'AGNEAU A L'ESTRAGON PRINTANIERE
(Saddle of Spring Lamb with Tarragon)

1 4¼-pound (2-kilogram) saddle of spring lamb
½ cup lard
¾ cup dry white wine
1 bouquet fresh tarragon, chopped
1 cup veal stock
3 tablespoons butter
Salt and freshly ground pepper to taste
6 small tomatoes, peeled
2 cups sliced potatoes
¼ cup green olives
2 cups sliced carrots
Butter
6 artichoke hearts
1 teaspoon lemon juice
1½ cups cut string beans
1½ cups fresh peas
½ cup butter
1 bunch watercress

Remove the skin from the saddle. Rub lard into skin and tie back over meat with string to act as a baster. Roast the saddle for 20 minutes in a hot (400° F.) oven. Remove the string, discard the skin and turn the saddle over.to cook 5 minutes longer.

Remove the saddle from the oven while it is still rare. Deglaze the roasting pan with the white wine and add the chopped tarragon. Boil down the wine by half. Mix the veal stock into wine and boil down again. Beat butter into the sauce. Add desired seasonings.

In the meantime grill the tomatoes, brown the potatoes with the olives, cook the carrots in water with butter and let them glaze when the water is entirely evaporated. Also cook the artichoke hearts in water with lemon juice. The string beans and peas should be cooked in boiling water, then buttered and separately seasoned.

Place the saddle in the middle of a large heated plate. Arrange the vegetables around it, taking care to make a pleasing presentation. Coat the saddle with the very hot sauce. Garnish with watercress.

Serves: 4

Wine: Côte du Rhone Gigondas or Bordeaux Saint Estéple

Taverna Ta Nissia, Athens Hilton Hotel
Athens, Greece
Chef: Manfred Bertele

SADDLE OF LAMB "TA NISSIA"

1 4½-pound (2.5-kilogram) saddle of lamb, cleaned and ready for oven
   Salt and freshly ground pepper to taste
   Thyme
3½ tablespoons olive oil
6 grape leaves
8 artichoke hearts
2 tablespoons butter, softened
   Salt and freshly ground pepper to taste
6 slices louza (raw, smoked) ham or cooked ham
½ cup red wine
6 mushroom caps, sautéed

Rub lamb with salt, pepper, thyme and ½ tablespoon oil. Cover with grape leaves and refrigerate for 8 to 10 hours. Heat 3 tablespoons oil in a roasting pan, remove leaves from lamb and place roast in pan in a moderately slow (325° F.) oven for about 45 minutes. When roast is done, set aside to cool.

While lamb is roasting, boil the artichoke hearts until tender, about 30 to 45 minutes, and put through a sieve. Mix with softened butter and heat in a small saucepan. Season with salt and pepper.

When lamb has cooled, remove meat from the bone and cut into ½-inch slices. Purée artichokes and spread on each slice; then lay half a slice of ham over it. Replace lamb slices on the bone to form original shape. Return lamb to roasting pan. Warm red wine and pour over lamb before returning it to oven for 5 minutes. Baste several times. Remove lamb to serving platter, strain the red wine gravy, check seasoning and pour over meat. Garnish with mushroom caps. Serve with rice pilaf or fried potatoes, grilled tomatoes and string beans, if desired.

Serves: 4

Wine: Cimarosa

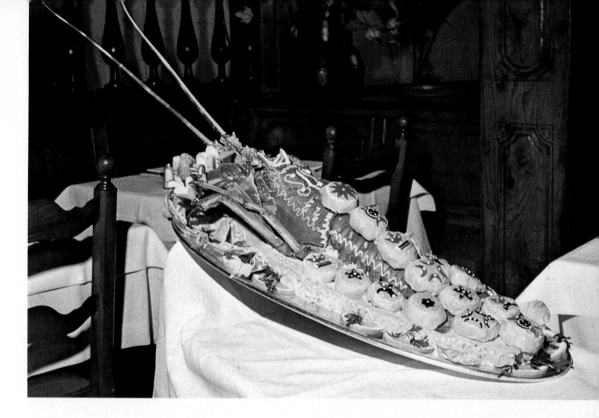

SABATINI
Florence, Italy
Chef: Francesco Focardi
Aragosta in Bellavista
(page 159)

de GRAVENMOLEN
Amsterdam, Netherlands
Chef: Alexander Koene
Filets de Sole aux Fruits de Mer
(page 129)

THE RUSSELL
Dublin, Ireland
Chef: Tony Butler
Le Croquembouche
(page 199)

La Rotonde

Luchon, France

Chef: Christian Es

LE PETERAM LUCHONNAIS

(Mutton with Calf's Feet)

- **1 mutton belly and 8 feet**
- **2 calf's feet**
- **2½ pounds (1.25 kilograms) calf's intestinal casing**
- **1 ham bone**
- **3 carrots**
- **Bouquet Garni (see index)**
- **1 teaspoon tomato paste**
- **½ cup diced ham**
- **2 slices bacon, diced**
- **1 clove garlic, chopped**
- **2 chopped onions**
- **Salt and freshly ground pepper to taste**
- **Dash nutmeg**
- **2 cups dry white wine**
- **1 pound potatoes, diced**

Blanch the belly and feet; then drop them into cold water. Scrape well. Cut the calf's intestinal casing into pieces 2 inches by 2 inches. Place all in a stew pan with ham bone. Add carrots, Bouquet Garni, tomato paste, ham, bacon, garlic, onion, salt, pepper and nutmeg. Pour in the white wine. Bring to a boil, cover and simmer on a low flame for about 10 hours. One hour before serving, add the diced potatoes.

Serves: 5 or 6

Wine: Madiran Racanel

Ristorante Rosati

Rome, Italy

Chef: Simioli

COSTOLETTE DI VITELLO "ROSATI"

(Cutlet of Veal)

- **1 veal cutlet**
- **2 tablespoons liver pâté**
- **2 tablespoons flour**
- **1 egg, beaten**
- **2 tablespoons butter**

Pound cutlet until uniformly thin and smooth. Put pâté on cutlet and fold. Pound edges together to seal. Dredge stuffed cutlet in flour, then dip in egg, then again in flour. Cook in butter about 15 minutes, turning once.

Serves: 1

Wine: Venegazzi red

Restaurant Gundel
Budapest, Hungary
Chef: Julius Pár

PAPRIKA VEAL

2 pounds (1 kilogram) shoulder of veal
½ cup finely chopped onions
6 tablespoons lard
½ teaspoon paprika
Salt to taste
2 small green peppers, chopped
2 small tomatoes, peeled, seeded and chopped
1 cup sour cream
1 tablespoon flour
1 teaspoon salt

Cut the meat into fairly large (2½-inch) cubes. Sauté the onion in lard until it is a light yellow; add the paprika and 2 tablespoons water and cook for 1 or 2 minutes. Add the meat, salt it and let it simmer covered, stirring from time to time and adding a little more water if necessary. When meat is nearly tender, add green peppers and tomatoes. Cook until vegetables are tender, then mix sour cream with flour and stir in. Cook, stirring, another 3 or 4 minutes. Should gravy be too thick, add a little water. Season with salt. Serve with dumplings or steamed rice, if desired.

Serves: 4

Wine: Chablis

Hotel Gellèrt
Budapest, Hungary
Chef: Ferenc Novák

VEAL CUTLET MAGYAROVAR

5 veal cutlets
1 tablespoon salt
¼ cup flour
¼ cup lard
1 cup finely chopped mushrooms
1 teaspoon fines herbes
5 slices ham
5 slices óvár cheese or mozzarella
4 cups boiled rice
½ cup cooked green peas
¾ cup beef, mushroom or veal-roast gravy
Potato chips

Pound cutlets until very thin. Salt and dredge lightly in flour. Brown quickly on both sides in hot lard. Set aside. Mix mushrooms with fines herbes. Spread mixture on cutlets and top with ham slice and then cheese slice. Drain all but 1 tablespoon of lard from skillet and return cutlets to cook until tender and cheese soft. Run skillet under broiler for a minute to slightly brown cheese.

To serve, mix rice and peas. Heat well. Place one serving of rice on each plate and top with cutlet. Pour hot gravy over meat and garnish plate with potato chips.

Serves: 5

Wine: Chablis

Hostaria dell'Orso

Rome, Italy

Chef: Senigallta

VEAL SCALLOPS WITH HAM AND CHEESE

10 slices raw ham
10 slices Gruyère cheese
3½ pounds (1.75 kilograms) veal (20 thin cutlets)
   Flour
½ cup butter
½ cup olive oil
¾ cup dry white wine
1½ tablespoons pâté de foie gras
¼ cup jus de viande*

Sandwich ham and cheese between each pair of veal slices. Cover the outside surfaces of each "sandwich" with flour. Place butter and oil in a pan and fry the meat in it for about 4 or 5 minutes. Add wine. When the slices have been removed from the pan, add the pâté de foie gras and jus de viande to the remaining juices. Let cook for a further 2 minutes and then pour this sauce over the veal.

Serves: 10

*Literally, meat juice; popularly, gravy from roast meat. If you do not have leftover gravy, canned beef gravy is a good substitute.

Wine: Red wine, not too old

Quadri

Venice, Italy

Chef: Giovanni Mellina

PICCATINA DI VITELLO ALLA LORD BYRON

(Highly Flavored Veal "Lord Byron")

2 tablespoons olive oil
¼ cup butter
8 veal scallops, thinly sliced and pounded
   Flour
1 tomato, peeled, seeded and chopped
1 teaspoon salt
½ cup dry white wine
1 cup mild chilies, cut into thin strips
½ teaspoon oregano
½ teaspoon fines herbes

Heat olive oil with butter until butter is completely melted. Dredge veal scallops in flour and sauté 5 minutes. Add tomato to skillet and let it cook with meat for 10 minutes. Sprinkle with salt and add white wine. Put the chilies, oregano and fines herbes into the pan and cook gently until the scallops are very tender—just another few minutes.

Serves: 4

Restaurant de Boerdery

Amsterdam, Netherlands

Chef: H. F. Wunneberg

STEAK DE VEAU DUXELLES

(Veal Steak with Mushrooms and Chicken Livers)

1½ pounds (750 grams) mushrooms
1½ pounds (750 grams) chicken livers
2 tablespoons butter
½ cup chopped onions
   Pinch garlic powder
1 bay leaf
   Freshly ground pepper to taste
   Pinch paprika
   Pinch thyme
2 tablespoons brandy
2 tablespoons dry white wine
¼ cup flour
1 cup veal stock
¼ cup heavy cream
4 ¼-pound (120-gram) veal steaks
¼ cup grated Gruyère cheese

Finely chop mushrooms and chicken livers and mix. Sauté in butter with chopped onion, garlic powder, bay leaf, pepper, paprika and thyme. Flame with brandy. Add white wine. Add flour and veal stock. Finish with cream. Put on one side to cool.

Lightly grill veal steaks. Then place duxelles on top and add grated cheese. Place in a warm (200° F.) oven for 5 minutes, or until cheese is bubbly.

Serves: 4

Wine: Château Trotanoy Pomerol (1961)

Collar of Gold Restaurant

Dublin Airport, Ireland

Chef: James Doyle

VEAL "COLLAR OF GOLD"

¼ cup butter
4 veal scallops
½ cup sliced button mushrooms
¼ cup chopped onion
2 cups sherry
5 cups heavy cream
   Salt and freshly ground pepper to taste
1 tablespoon chopped parsley

Clarify butter in frying pan. Add veal, brown and set aside. Sauté mushrooms and onion in pan juices; add sherry and cream. Reduce sauce until thickened and season. Return veal to pan and heat through. Sprinkle with chopped parsley and serve.

Serves: 4

Wine: Claret

Leoni's Quo Vadis

London, England

ESCALOPPA DEL MAITRE

(Veal Scallops with Ham and Cheese)

- 4 **5-ounce (150-gram) veal scallops**
- 1 **tablespoon olive oil**
  Salt and freshly ground pepper to taste
- 8 **1-ounce (30-gram) slices Bel Paese cheese**
- 4 **2-ounce (60-gram) slices Parma ham**
- 1 **cup button mushrooms**
- ½ **cup tomato sauce**

Brown veal in oil for about 3 minutes on each side. Sprinkle with salt and pepper. Remove from flame. On top of each scallop, place a slice of cheese, ham and cheese again. Return to flame. When cheese begins to melt slightly, add mushrooms and tomato sauce. Simmer for a few minutes. Serve very hot.

Serves: 4

Wine: Bolla Valpolicella

Welcombe Hotel

Stratford-upon-Avon, England

Chef: J. M. Vallade

ESCALOPE DE VEAU VAUCANSON

(Veal Scallops with Tomatoes)

- 4 **½-pound (250-gram) veal scallops**
  Salt and freshly ground pepper to taste
- 2 **tablespoons sweet butter**
- ¼ **cup chopped onion**
- 1 **cup peeled, seeded and chopped tomatoes**
- 2 **tablespoons chopped parsley**
- 1 **tablespoon brandy**
- 2 **cups heavy cream**
  Chopped parsley

Season veal with salt and pepper. Melt butter in skillet and sauté veal until golden brown. Remove from skillet to a serving platter and keep warm. Add onion, tomatoes and parsley to the skillet. Cook gently for 5 minutes. Add brandy and reduce to about ½ cup, or until mixture is rather thick. Add cream and simmer for 5 minutes. Taste for seasoning. Pour sauce over veal, sprinkle with parsley and serve immediately.

Serves: 4

Wine: Corton-Charlemagne 1964

Lorensberg Restaurant
Göteborg, Sweden
Chef: Allan Hult

FILLET OF VEAL KARL GERHARD

  4 ¼-pound (120-gram) veal scallops
    Salt and freshly ground pepper to taste
  5 tablespoons flour
  1 teaspoon curry powder
  3 tablespoons butter
  3 tablespoons cognac
  ½ cup sherry
1⅓ cups veal stock
  ¼ cup butter
    Hot pepper sauce
  2 cups sliced mushrooms
  2 tablespoons butter
  4 pieces cooked lobster meat
2½ cups cooked rice
  ½ cup coarsely chopped red pepper
  ½ cup coarsely chopped green pepper

Pound veal scallops thin; season with salt and pepper. Dredge in flour mixed with curry powder. Sauté scallops in 3 tablespoons butter until golden brown. Pour cognac over meat and flame. Remove and keep warm. Pour sherry and veal stock into cooking pan and boil for a few minutes. Stir in ¼ cup butter. Season with a few drops hot pepper sauce; sauté mushrooms in 2 tablespoons of butter and add. Pour sauce over scallops and place piece of lobster on top of each. Serve accompanied by rice and mixed raw peppers.
Serves: 4

Carlton Tower Hotel
London, England
Chef: Bernard Gaume

ESCALOPES DE VEAU DAUPHINOISE
(Veal Scallops with Ham and Mushrooms)

  8 small thin veal scallops
    Salt and freshly ground pepper to taste
  2 tablespoons butter
1¼ cups sliced mushrooms
  ¼ cup dry white wine
  ½ cup heavy cream
  1 cup julienne cooked ham
  3 tablespoons grated Gruyère cheese
  1 egg yolk, lightly beaten

Season veal with salt and pepper. Sauté each side 3 or 4 minutes in butter until both sides are lightly browned. Remove to a round serving dish, arranging them in the form of a crown. Keep warm.

To make the sauce, use the same pan. Quickly cook sliced mushrooms with white wine and cream. Reduce to desired consistency. Add ham and grated cheese. Remove from heat and add egg yolk. Stir well. Check seasoning and pour sauce over scallops. Glaze in a hot (400° F.) oven.
Serves: 4

Wine: White Burgundy

Four Seasons and Vintage Room
London, England
Chef: R. Bellone

SADDLE OF VEAL ORLOFF

**1 12-pound (6-kilogram) saddle of veal
Salt and freshly ground pepper to taste**

Season veal with salt and pepper. Roast in a moderate (350° F.) oven for about 1½ hours, or until meat thermometer registers 170° F. and juices run pale yellow when pricked with a fork. When done, set aside to cool. Reserve meat juices.

Duxelles

**½ cup finely chopped onions
4 cups finely chopped mushrooms
¼ cup butter**

Sauté onions and mushrooms in butter until very soft—almost mushy. Set aside.

Soubise Sauce

**¼ cup rice, blanched for 5 minutes in salted water
1 cup minced onions
1 cup white stock
½ cup butter
1 cup flour
2½ cups boiling milk
Meat juices from veal
½ cup heavy cream
4 egg yolks, beaten
¼ cup butter**

In a large saucepan, cook rice and onions in stock for 30 minutes. Pound in a mortar and pass through a fine sieve. While rice and onions are cooking, make a roux with butter and flour. Pour in milk to which meat juices have been added. Mix until smooth. Add ¼ cup cream and beat until sauce is thick enough to coat a spoon. Add the soubise; mix thoroughly. Beat in egg yolks. Do not allow to boil, but heat gently until all ingredients are thoroughly blended. Beat in remaining cream. Sauce should be very thick. Remove from heat and whip in butter by the spoonful.

Conclusion

**Saddle of veal
½ cup onion purée
Duxelles
1 cup pâté de foie gras, finely sliced
Soubise Sauce
¼ cup grated Gruyère cheese**

Remove meat from the bone, cutting in diagonal slices about ¼ inch thick. Spread on each slice the onion purée and Duxelles and a slice of pâté. Replace veal slices in original saddle shape on a long, heatproof serving dish. Pour Soubise Sauce over the veal, sprinkle with cheese and glaze in a hot (450° F.) oven for about 5 minutes, or until sauce begins to brown and cheese is melted.

Serves: 15

Wine: Domaine de Chevalier, Graves Château 1959

Churchill Hotel

London, England

COTE DE VEAU A LA BONNE FEMME
(Veal Chops with Bacon)

  2 cups small onions
½ cup white stock or water
½ cup butter
  4 ½-pound (250-gram) veal chops
     Salt and freshly ground pepper to taste
  1 tablespoon flour
  1 cup cubed and blanched lean bacon
½ cup button mushrooms
  2 cups sliced potatoes
¾ cup jus lié (starch-thickened meat juices)
  1 tablespoon chopped parsley

Braise onions in stock or water, 2 tablespoons butter and salt and pepper for about 40 minutes. While onions are cooking, season the chops with salt and pepper. Rub well with flour. Melt 2 tablespoons butter in a skillet and brown the chops, about 8 minutes on each side. Set aside. If necessary, add 1 tablespoon butter to skillet and quickly fry bacon. Set aside. Add another tablespoon butter, if necessary, and quickly sauté mushrooms. Set aside. Sauté potatoes in the same skillet, adding remaining butter, if necessary. Making sure not to let the potatoes stick, continuously roll them around the pan to brown them lightly on all sides. This will take about 15 minutes.

Place chops on heatproof serving dish and decorate each chop with six onions, six cubes bacon and six potato slices. Place some mushrooms on top of each chop. Place in hot (450° F.) oven for about 5 minutes to warm through. Pour a ladle of jus lié around outside of dish and sprinkle with parsley.

Serves: 4

Wine: Meursault 1962

Old Swiss House

Lucerne, Switzerland

Chef: Claus Hemmann

VEAL SCALLOPS VALAISANNE

  2 thin slices veal
  1 tablespoon flour
¼ cup butter
  1 tablespoon dry white wine
  1 peeled tomato, cut in 3 slices
  2 slices Tilsiter or other firm Swiss cheese

Dust veal slices with flour and sauté in butter. Remove meat and keep warm. Add white wine and tomato slices to pan. When tomato slices are hot, put on top of meat. Cover with cheese slices and heat in a moderately hot (375° F.) oven until cheese has melted, about 10 minutes. Serve with noodles or hashed-brown potatoes, if desired.

Serves: 1

Wine: White wine or rosé

Hunting Lodge
London, England
Chef: H. P. Lullier

SADDLE OF VEAL

(A Delicacy of the Sixteenth Century)

- **1 saddle of veal**
- **1 teaspoon thyme**
- **½ cup chopped carrots**
- **1 onion, sliced**
- **Quenelles (recipe follows)**
- **½ cup mead or dark beer or ale**

Rub veal with thyme and roast in a moderately slow (300° F.) oven for 40 to 45 minutes per pound with carrots and onion. When cooked, remove from oven and let stand 20 minutes before carving. Garnish platter with Quenelles, small boiled cucumbers and asparagus.

To make gravy, deglaze the roasting pan with mead. Reduce the pan juices until thick, then pass through a fine sieve. Discard carrots and onion. When saddle is carved, pour meat juices that run out into the gravy. Heat through and pour over meat. Serve with Jerusalem artichokes and French beans, if desired.

Quenelles

- **2 cups boned pike pieces**
- **½ cup heavy cream**
- **3 egg whites**
- **Mace**
- **12 tiny peeled cucumbers**
- **½ cup sliced asparagus**

Pound the pike in a mortar and mix in cream and egg whites. Flavor with mace.

Chill. Mold quenelles with two spoons and poach in salted water with cucumbers and asparagus. When quenelles are firm, remove with a slotted spoon, drain and keep warm.

Serves: 4 to 6

Gresham Hotel
Dublin, Ireland
Chef: Michael McManus

ESCALOPE OF VEAL MAISON

(Veal Scallop Gresham)

- **1 veal scallop**
- **1 egg, beaten**
- **2 tablespoons bread crumbs**
- **Salt and freshly ground pepper to taste**
- **1 teaspoon olive oil**
- **¼ cup finely chopped onion**
- **1 tomato, peeled, seeded and chopped**
- **2 tablespoons heavy cream**
- **1 tablespoon grated Parmesan cheese**
- **1 egg yolk**
- **1 tablespoon butter, melted**

Dip veal in egg, then in bread crumbs and season to taste with salt and pepper. Sauté veal in olive oil 3 to 4 minutes a side, or until cooked through. Keep warm.

To make sauce, sauté the onion; add tomato and cream. Cook 5 minutes. Pour over veal. Add cheese to egg yolk. Beat with melted butter until thick. Coat veal with tomato mixture and glaze under broiler. Garnish with croquette potatoes and stuffed tomatoes, if desired.

Serves: 1

Wine: White Bordeaux

Lafayette
Dublin, Ireland
Chef: Roger Hoblet

ROSETTES DE VEAU PARISIENNE
(Veal Scallops with Truffles)

¼ cup coarsely chopped onion
¼ cup coarsely chopped carrots
½ cup coarsely chopped celery
¼ cup butter
½ cup sherry
1 cup veal stock
 Salt and freshly ground pepper to taste
 Thyme
1 bay leaf
2 tablespoons flour
2 tablespoons butter
2 truffles, finely chopped
1 cup mushrooms, finely chopped
1 teaspoon lemon juice
 Salt and freshly ground pepper to taste
1¼ cups heavy cream
8 veal cutlets, pounded thin
2 tablespoons olive oil
2 tablespoons butter
 Potatoes Parisienne (recipe follows)

Cook onion, carrot and celery slowly in butter in a large saucepan for 10 minutes. Add sherry, veal stock, salt and pepper, thyme and bay leaf. Bring to boil and simmer for 35 minutes. Strain and thicken with 1 tablespoon flour and 1 tablespoon butter blended together. Add truffles and check seasonings.

Cook mushrooms very gently in a saucepan with lemon juice, salt, pepper and cream for 10 minutes. Bring to a boil; reduce the flame and simmer for 10 min-utes. Thicken with 1 tablespoon flour and 1 tablespoon butter blended together.

Sauté veal cutlets in oil and butter. When cooked, place four cutlets on a silver dish, cover with mushrooms and place other four cutlets on top. Place potatoes in center of dish, pour sauce over veal and serve.

Potatoes Parisienne

2 dozen small new potatoes, peeled
¼ cup chopped onion
¼ cup minced green pepper
½ cup butter
 Salt

Cook potatoes in boiling salted water until tender. Meanwhile, sauté the onion and green pepper in half the butter until soft. Add drained and cooked potatoes and the rest of the butter. Stir gently to coat potatoes. Sprinkle with salt.

Serves: 4

Wine: Nuits-Saint-Georges 1966

The Mirabeau
Dun Laóghaire, County Dublin
Ireland
Chef: Patrick Rafferty

ESCALOPES DE TERNERA A LA VALENCIA

(Veal Scallops Valencia)

12 paper-thin slices ham
12 veal scallops
¼ cup Spanish or other olive oil
   Salt and freshly ground pepper to taste
1 medium onion, finely chopped
2 orange peels, grated
1 cup orange juice
½ cup amontillado sherry
1 teaspoon cornstarch
1 orange, sectioned
½ cup chopped parsley

Place a slice of ham over each slice of veal, pound together with a mallet, roll up and fasten with a toothpick. Brown quickly in olive oil, sprinkling with salt and pepper as they brown. Add onion, grated peel, orange juice and sherry to the pan. Cover and cook for 20 to 25 minutes. Remove meat to platter; thicken sauce with cornstarch and adjust seasonings. Pour sauce over veal. Serve garnished with orange sections and chopped parsley.

Serves: 6

Wine: Bernkasteler Green Label

La Sangria
Charbonnières-les-Bains, France
Chef: Michel Lorrain

ESCALOPES DE VEAU CORDON ROUGE

(Veal Scallops Cordon Rouge)

8 top round veal cutlets
   Salt
   Paprika
4 thin slices Gruyère cheese
2 slices boiled ham
   Salt
½ cup flour
2 eggs, beaten
1¼ cups fresh bread crumbs
2 tablespoons butter
4 slices truffle
1 pound (500 grams) asparagus, steamed in butter
1¼ cups pan-fried potato slices

Season four of the cutlets with salt and paprika. Top each with half a slice of Gruyère cheese, then half a slice of ham, then the rest of the Gruyère. Season again with paprika. Cover with the remaining four pieces of veal.

Press down edges of the veal "sandwiches" with your fingertips. Salt lightly. Dredge in flour, then dip into beaten egg, then into the fresh bread crumbs. Tap the filled scallops with the blade of a large kitchen knife to make the surplus crumbs fall off.

Sauté in a large pan with butter. Serve with truffle slices, asparagus and potato slices. Pour the pan juices over all.

Serves: 4

Wine: Pouilly-Fumé

Seehaus

Zürich, Switzerland

Chef: H. Rudolph

DILLED VEAL SCALLOPS WITH NOODLES SEEHAUS

6 thin slices veal

2 tablespoons butter

2 tablespoons cognac

1 tablespoon chopped dillweed

1 tablespoon chopped parsley

½ teaspoon paprika

½ teaspoon Worcestershire sauce

6 tablespoons veal gravy

6 tablespoons heavy cream

1 teaspoon lemon juice

Salt and freshly ground pepper to taste

Noodles Seehaus (recipe follows)

Sauté veal slices briefly in butter; flame with cognac. Add dillweed, parsley, paprika and Worcestershire sauce. Simmer for a few minutes. Remove veal from heat and keep warm. Sieve herbs remaining in the pan and let stand while making the sauce. Mix veal gravy, cream and lemon juice together. Add reserved ingredients; heat, stirring, until smooth. Season with salt and pepper.

Mound noodles on a platter. Arrange veal slices on noodles and top with sauce. Serve extra sauce separately.

Noodles Seehaus

1 cup flour

2 eggs

¼ cup cooked, chopped, drained spinach

2 tablespoons butter

¼ cup grated Parmesan cheese

½ cup heavy cream, whipped

Salt and freshly ground pepper to taste

Mix flour, eggs and spinach into a firm paste. Roll dough out and cut into ½-inch-wide noodle strips. Let dry at least 1 hour. Cook in a large pot of boiling salted water about 10 minutes, or just until tender. Drain. Dress noodles with butter, cheese and whipped cream; toss to coat. Season with salt and pepper.

Serves: 2

Wine: Pinot Noir "les Mazots"

Five Flies

Amsterdam, Netherlands

DUTCH VEAL STEAK WITH CHERRIES AND RAISINS

1 small veal steak

¼ cup butter

1 teaspoon paprika

1 tablespoon heavy cream

1 tablespoon raisins, soaked 5 minutes in boiling water

1 cup cherries, pitted

Fry veal steak in butter until brown on both sides. Add paprika. When steak is nearly cooked, add cream, raisins and cherries. Cook gently for another 5 to 6 minutes before serving.

Serves: 1

Wine: Rosé or Burgundy

On the Rocks
Varkiza, Athens, Greece
Chef: Nicolas Loudaras

Alcron
Prague, Czechoslovakia
Chef: M. Hribek

VEAL CUTLETS ON THE ROCKS

½ cup thinly sliced boiled ham
½ cup sliced mushrooms
8 2½-ounce (75-gram) veal cutlets
    Salt and freshly ground pepper to taste
2 tablespoons flour
2 tablespoons butter
2 tablespoons oil
    Sauce (recipe follows)

Place ham and mushrooms on four veal slices, salt and pepper and cover with remaining veal. Sprinkle the tops of each with flour. Heat butter and oil in skillet until almost smoking and sauté veal for about 4 to 5 minutes on each side, or until lightly browned. Place in a heatproof casserole, cover with reduced Sauce and bake in a moderate (350° F.) oven for about 8 minutes.

Sauce

2 tablespoons white meat stock
½ cup red wine (Naoussa Boutari)
2 tablespoons tomato sauce
1 tablespoon Worcestershire sauce

Remove excess fat from sauté pan. Add meat stock and wine, bring to a boil, scraping up coagulated juices. Add tomato sauce and Worcestershire sauce and reduce to about ⅓ cup.

Serves: 4

FILLED SLICE OF VEAL ALCRON

2 ½-pound (250-gram) slices veal roast
1 set veal brains
1¼ cups mushrooms, sliced
½ cup butter
10 eggs
½ cup flour
2 tablespoons salt
½ cup oil

Pound veal slices until very thin.

Remove veins and tough membranes from brains. Soak in cold salted water 30 minutes. Drain, dry thoroughly and cut into ½-inch pieces. Lightly sauté brains and mushrooms in butter. Beat eggs and add to pan just to heat through (do not let eggs set).

Place one veal slice in an oiled shallow heatproof pan. Top with filling and other slice of meat. Pound edges of slices with a meat mallet to seal. Sprinkle meat with flour and salt and brown in some of the oil. Turn carefully to brown other side. Add more oil as necessary. Bake in a moderate (350° F.) oven for 30 minutes, or until veal is tender and filling firm. Serve hot with boiled potatoes and mixed salad, if desired.

Serves: 10

Wine: Rouge de Grèce "Naoussa Boutari"

31 al Vicario
Rome, Italy
Chef: Suardi

NODINO "EL AL VICARIO"

  1 knuckle (nodino) of veal
  1 tablespoon flour
  ¼ cup butter
  2 tablespoons chopped boiled ham
  ¼ cup sliced mushrooms
  2 or 3 slices truffle
  2 tablespoons diced fontina cheese

Dredge the veal in flour and sauté in 2 tablespoons butter for 15 minutes. Meanwhile, cook ham, mushrooms and truffle in remaining butter in another pan. Then, place all ingredients in a greaseproof paper bag, adding the fontina cheese. Seal the bag and place in a hot (400° F.) oven for 5 or 6 minutes.

Serves: 1

Wine: Barbaresco 1964

La Couronne
Brussels, Belgium
Chef: M. Hulsens

ROGNONS DE VEAU A LA GUEUZE
(Veal Kidneys in Beer)

     2 veal kidneys, cleaned
  1½ cups gueuze*
     ½ cup shallots, chopped
     1 cup heavy cream
     1 teaspoon dry mustard
       Pinch chopped tarragon
     1 egg yolk
     2 tablespoons cognac

Cut the kidneys into slices about ½ inch thick and put to soak in cold water to cover. Simmer beer with chopped shallots until reduced to ¼ cup; add cream and cook until sauce is thick and smooth. Strain sauce through a fine sieve; add mustard, tarragon, egg yolk and cognac and mix well. Poach kidneys just until tender (do not overcook). Drain, arrange on hot serving dish and cover with sauce.

Serves: 2

*A slightly sparkling Belgian beer. Light lager works well.

Wine: Red Bordeaux or beer

Le Relais, Cafe Royal
London, England
Chef: G. Mouilleron

ROGNONS DE VEAU FLAMBE

(Veal Kidneys Flambé)

  1 veal kidney
 ¼ cup butter
    Salt and freshly ground pepper to taste
 ¼ cup brandy
 ½ cup dry white wine
 ½ cup thickened veal stock
  1 teaspoon French mustard
  1 teaspoon ground nutmeg
  1 teaspoon chopped parsley

Remove skin, outer covering and all fat from kidney, and cut into 1-inch cubes. Melt half the butter in sauté pan and when it starts to brown, add kidney. Season with salt and pepper and sauté 3 minutes. Add brandy and flame.

Remove sautéed kidney; place in a serving dish and keep warm. Pour white wine into sauté pan and reduce until almost evaporated. Add veal stock and boil for 1 minute. Remove from heat and work in the rest of the butter, the mustard and the nutmeg. Pour sauce over kidneys. Sprinkle with parsley and serve.

Serves: 2

Wine: Mouton Baron Philippe 1964

Athénée Palace
Bucharest, Romania
Chef: Constantin Tutila

SKEWERED MEAT "ATHENEE PALACE"

 ¾ pound (375 grams) fillet of pork
 ¾ pound (375 grams) sirloin of beef
 ¾ pound (375 grams) veal kidney
 ¾ pound (375 grams) pork kidney
  1 cup sliced onions
 ⅔ cup olive oil
  1 tablespoon salt
    Pinch freshly ground black pepper
    Pinch thyme
    Pinch basil
  2 tablespoons savory
 1¼ cups mushrooms
    Salt
 ½ cup lemon juice
 ⅔ cup sliced smoked bacon

Cut meat into cubes of about 1 inch (1 ounce). Place in bowl with onion, oil, salt, pepper, thyme, basil and savory. Cover and refrigerate for 12 hours.

In a covered saucepan, poach mushrooms with salt and lemon juice for 10 to 15 minutes.

On a skewer, place a cube of meat, a mushroom and a bacon slice, continuing to alternate until skewer is filled or all ingredients are used. Grill on a very hot grill, 3 minutes on each side. Serve with buttered vegetables or boiled rice, if desired.

Serves: 4

Dikker & Thijs
Amsterdam, Netherlands
Chef: Jean Otte

VEAL SWEETBREADS QUEEN JULIANA

- 1 pair veal sweetbreads
- Salt
- Fresh lemon juice
- 2 tablespoons chopped onion
- 2 tablespoons chopped parsley
- 2 tablespoons chopped celery
- 2 tablespoons chopped carrots
- ¼ cup butter
- 1 bay leaf
- 1 whole clove
- 10 peppercorns
- 2 cups beef tea (bouillon)
- 1 cup red wine
- 2 teaspoons flour
- 2 teaspoons butter
- ¼ cup Madeira
- 4 teaspoons butter
- ½ cup sliced mushrooms
- 6 tablespoons minced ox tongue
- 6 tablespoons chopped ham
- 3 tablespoons chopped truffles
- 2 cups goose liver pâté, sliced
- 1 cup haricot beans
- 1 cup potato croquettes

Soak sweetbreads in cold water for 30 minutes. Remove membranes. Poach sweetbreads for 15 minutes in water to cover to which has been added 1 teaspoon salt and 1 teaspoon lemon juice for each ¼ cup. Cool.

To make the sauce, brown the vegetables in ¼ cup butter, add bay leaf and spices, beef tea and red wine. Cook for 30 minutes. Brown 2 teaspoons flour with 2 teaspoons butter and add to sauce to thicken. When sauce is thick, pass through fine sieve and flavor with Madeira.

Melt 4 teaspoons butter, brown the sweetbreads and slowly bake for 10 minutes in a closed pot. Add sliced mushrooms, ox tongue, ham, truffles and sauce.

Before serving, cover sweetbreads with slices of goose liver pâté. It will melt and cover sweetbreads. Garnish with haricot beans and croquette potatoes.

Serves: 4

Wine: Château Smith Haut Lafitte 1922—Martillac

Le Coq d'Or
London, England
Chef: J. C. Besnier

LA CASSOLETTE DE RIS DE VEAU "BENEDICT"

(Braised Sweetbreads with Morels)

2 pairs calf's sweetbreads
½ cup dry white wine
¼ cup chopped carrots
¼ cup chopped onion
2 shallots, chopped
3 tablespoons heavy cream
1 cup fresh morels or ¼ cup dry morels, cooked

Braise sweetbreads with white wine, carrots, onion and shallots. Remove sweetbreads and keep warm. Reduce stock by half, strain and combine with cream to make velouté sauce (white sauce). Just heat through. Flake sweetbreads into small pieces and mix with morels and the sauce. Serve in cassolette made of short flaky pastry, if desired.

Serves: 4

Wine: Chablis

Mirabelle
London, England
Chef: John Drees

CASSOLETTE DE RIS DE VEAU

(Casserole of Sweetbreads)

1 cup puff pastry
½ cup any dry beans
1½ pounds (750 grams) calf's sweetbreads
¾ cup butter
Salt and freshly ground pepper to taste
½ cup dry white wine
¼ cup dry sherry
¾ cup heavy cream
Pinch saffron
¼ cup pâté de fois gras

Roll puff pastry thin and place in four 4-inch tart molds. Fill with dry beans and cook in hot (400° F.) oven for about 12 minutes. Discard beans. Keep pastries warm. Cover sweetbreads with cold salted water; bring to boil and cook 5 minutes. Remove from heat and rinse in cold water. Put sweetbreads in saucepan with half the butter, salt and pepper, and cook for 5 minutes on each side. Then add wine, sherry, cream and saffron; cook for 15 minutes over medium heat.

Remove sweetbreads and place in pastry shells. Cut pâté de foie gras in very small pieces and add to sauce, mixing well. Add the rest of butter. Pour sauce over sweetbreads and serve.

Serves: 4

Wine: Château Beychevelle

Das Alte Haus "Delevo"
Innsbruck, Austria
Chef: Rûdiger Pischl

PAELLA MADRILENA

½ cup small pieces fillet of pork
3 serving pieces chicken
  Thyme
  Sage
  Salt and freshly ground pepper to taste
3 tablespoons olive oil
2 tablespoons chopped onion
¼ cup chopped green pepper
¼ cup diced ham
4 strips bacon, chopped
⅓ cup red wine
1 cup peeled, cooked tomatoes
2½ cups light stock or salted water
1¼ cups long-grained rice
½ teaspoon saffron
¼ cup flaked crab meat
6 shrimp
  Oil
1 cup cooked, flaked whitefish
4 green olives
6 mussels in shells
  French-Fried Parsley (recipe follows)

Season pork and chicken with herbs and salt and pepper. Sauté very lightly in olive oil. Add onion, pepper, ham and bacon and cook until onion is wilted. Add wine and cook until liquid is reduced by half. Stir in tomatoes and check seasonings.

Bring stock or salted water to a boil. Pour in rice and stir saffron through. Cover tightly and cook over lowest heat for about 30 minutes. The rice should be tender but not soft and all the liquid should have been absorbed.

Sauté crab meat and shrimp in a little oil. In a large shallow heatproof dish, mix rice, flaked fish, crab meat, shrimp and olives. Pour the tomato-meat mixture over the rice. Arrange mussels on top of dish and bake in a moderately hot (375° F.) oven for about 10 minutes, or just until the mussels open. (Discard any that do not open.) Garnish with French-Fried Parsley.

French-Fried Parsley

1 small bunch fresh parsley
  Vegetable oil

Wash parsley well ahead of time and dry *thoroughly*. Separate bunch into small bundles of 2 or 3 sprigs each. Parsley stems or cooking twine should bind the bundles securely. Heat enough vegetable oil to completely cover the parsley to 360° F. Cook parsley a few seconds only. Drain. (Remove string if it was used to tie bunches.) Use as garnish.

Serves: 3

Wine: Châteauneuf-du-Pape

Capucin Gourmand

Nancy, France

Chef: Maitrejean

GRILLADES DE PORC "DIJONNAISE"
(Grilled Pork)

- 4 pork cutlets
- 2 tablespoons butter
- 1 cup heavy cream
- 6 pickled gherkins, sliced
- 2 tablespoons white mustard
- 1 tablespoon wine vinegar
- 1 tablespoon chopped shallot
- Salt and freshly ground pepper to taste

Fry the pork in the butter. While it cooks, combine cream in a bowl with gherkins, mustard, vinegar, shallot, salt and pepper; blend thoroughly.

When the grillades are done, remove them to a serving platter and keep them warm. Pour the fat off the pan and add the prepared mixture. Boil 2 minutes. Pour over the grillades and serve.

Serves: 4

Wine: Saint Embion (Bordeaux)

Royal Hotel

Copenhagen, Denmark

Chef: Mogens Bech Andersen

ROAST PORK WITH CRACKLINGS

- 2 or 3 pounds (1 kilogram or more) neck of pork, with rind
- Salt

Preheat oven to very hot (475° F.). Deeply score the pork rind. Place meat with rind down in a shallow roasting pan. Add as much boiling water as is needed to cover rind, and boil on top of the stove for 20 minutes. Turn meat so that rind is uppermost and rub salt well into rind. Place a meat thermometer in middle of the meat and put it in the oven for about 25 minutes, or until rind starts to bubble. Reduce heat to moderately slow (300° F.) and let the meat roast for about 45 minutes, or until thermometer shows 170° F. Switch off heat and cover roast slightly, leaving it in oven for about 10 to 15 minutes to allow juices to permeate the meat before carving. Serve with red cabbage and candied sweet potatoes, if desired.

Serves: 4 or 6

Restaurante Botin
Madrid, Spain
Chef: Hilario Gutierrez

ROAST SUCKING PIG

1 10-pound (5-kilogram) sucking pig
2 bay leaves
1 sprig parsley
2 cloves garlic
1 sprig thyme
¼ cup chopped onion
1 cup lard or shortening
  Salt
  Paprika
1 cup dry white wine

Cut lengthwise almost through the sucking pig and clean. Then spread it flat with opened side up in a roasting pan. Chop bay leaves, parsley, garlic and thyme, add to onion and sprinkle on meat. Rub all over with lard or shortening. Season with salt and paprika. Add white wine and 4 cups water to the pan and place in a hot (400° F.) oven for an hour. Then remove excess liquid and fat and replace pan in oven for another 20 minutes with skin side up. Baste skin with pan juices and put back in oven for another 30 minutes, or until the skin is golden brown and crisp.

Serves: 6

Wine: Valdepeñas red

Jadran
Dubrovnik, Yugoslavia
Chef: Stijepo Turanjanin

CEVAP*

(Skewered Meats, Bandit-Style)

¼ cup olive oil
1¾ pounds (875 grams) pork, veal, beef, liver and smoked bacon, cut in 1-inch cubes
3¼ cups mixed vegetables
3½ tablespoons butter
1¾ cups boiled rice

Rub oil on all meats and place on one large skewer or individual skewers, alternating the varieties. Grill (or broil) about 7 minutes on each side, or until all meats are done. Prepare the vegetables according to type used, drain well and add the butter. Place meat on serving platter and garnish with the vegetables and the rice. If individual skewers are used, pass the vegetables and rice separately.

Serves: 5

*This is a very rich and popular dish, descending from the days of the bandits in the early eighteenth century.

Wine: Dingač

Glebe Hotel
Barford (near Warwick), England
Chef: Alan Crane

SWEET ROAST LOIN OF PORK GLEBE

1 3½-pound (1.75-kilogram) loin of pork, boned
¾ cup butter
¼ cup julienne carrots
¼ cup julienne turnips
¼ cup julienne parsnips
¼ cup julienne rutabaga
¼ cup julienne leeks
¼ cup flour
2 cups sauce Espagnole (available ready-made) or brown stock
1 tablespoon wine vinegar
Salt
¼ cup sugar
1¼ cups light ale
4 tomatoes, broiled
1 head cauliflower, boiled
1 cup rice, cooked
1 tablespoon slivered red pimientos
1 cup creamed potatoes

Roast pork in moderately hot (375° F.) oven for 1½ hours. Remove to an oval serving platter and keep warm.

Heat butter in a skillet and sauté the julienne for about 10 minutes, or until vegetables are coated and become soft.

In a saucepan, make a roux with flour and about 2 tablespoons of fat from the roast pork. Bring brown stock to a boil and beat into roux until sauce is smooth. Simmer until the sauce is thick enough to coat a spoon. Add vinegar and salt. Set aside.

Caramelize sugar with 1 tablespoon butter drawn from butter in which vegetables were cooked. Deglaze with ale, add sauce and simmer until mixture is thoroughly blended. To this add the julienne. Carve pork and cover with the sauce and vegetables. Garnish with tomatoes, cauliflower, rice, pimientos and creamed potatoes.

Serves: 4

Wine: Rosé d'Anjou (Clos du Lauon)

117

Section Seven

FISH AND SHELLFISH

Hotel Marski

Helsinki, Finland

Chef: Leo Lampi

SOLE ROLLS STUFFED WITH MORELS

1 cup puff pastry

1¾ cups morels or mushrooms

1 teaspoon salt

2 tablespoons butter

Heavy cream

Salt and freshly ground pepper to taste

4½ pounds (2.25 kilograms) sole fillets

5½ tablespoons sliced onion

Salt and freshly ground pepper to taste

3½ tablespoons butter

6 tablespoons dry white wine

Make fleurons by rolling puff pastry out on a lightly floured board to about a ¼-inch thickness. With a fluted pastry cutter, cut out four crescents and place on cookie sheet lined with wax paper. Refrigerate for 30 minutes.

Cut mushrooms lengthwise, rinse in cold water and soak for 5 minutes in 1 quart of water and salt. Drain and dry thoroughly. Melt butter in skillet and sauté morels over medium heat until all juice is absorbed. Stir in cream by the tablespoon to make a thick paste. Season with salt and pepper and set aside.

Loosely roll fillets, leaving space for stuffing. Place rolled fillets in a buttered heatproof serving dish over the sliced onion. Salt and pepper to taste, and dot with butter. Add wine; cover with kitchen parchment or foil and bake in a moderate (350° F.) oven for about 15 minutes.

Conclusion

1 egg, lightly beaten

2 tablespoons heavy cream

4 fleurons

Sole fillets

Morel stuffing

1¾ cups Hollandaise Sauce (see index)

2 cups Duchesse Potatoes (see index)

4 sprigs dillweed

Beat egg with cream and brush tops of fleurons with it. Bake in a hot (400° F.) oven for 20 minutes. Meanwhile, stuff rolled fillets with morel stuffing and return to heatproof serving dish. Cover with Hollandaise Sauce and return to oven for about 5 minutes, or until sauce is bubbling. Arrange Duchesse Potatoes around the fish and the baked fleurons around the potatoes. Decorate with dillweed.

Serves: 4

Wine: Chablis

Wheeler's Sovereign
London, England
Chef: Man Ying Sau

SOLE POMMERY

- 4 1-pound (500-gram) Dover or other available soles
- ¼ cup flour
- 1 cup butter
- 2 lemons, halved
  Salt and freshly ground pepper to taste
- 1 cup peeled, cored and sliced table apples
- 4 teaspoons mango chutney

Wash fish and cut off heads and small bones around edges. Remove both the white and dark skin. Dip fish in flour. Melt ½ cup butter in a skillet and sauté the fish in it over low heat for about 10 minutes on each side. When nearly done, squeeze lemon juice over them and simmer for about 5 minutes. Season with salt and pepper.

Melt ½ cup butter in another skillet and very gently sauté apples in it until light brown. When fish is done, place on serving platter. Arrange apple slices on top and chutney at the side. Pour butter in which fish was cooked over the top and serve immediately.

Serves: 4

Wine: Puligny-Montrachet les Folatières 1967

Ivy Restaurant
London, England
Chef: Leon

JULIENNE MARYLAND

- 1 2-pound (1-kilogram) sole, filleted
- 1 tablespoon flour
- 1 egg, beaten
- 1 tablespoon bread crumbs
- 1 large sweet potato
  Salt and freshly ground pepper to taste
- 2 firm bananas
- 2 tablespoons oil
- 1 orange, closely peeled
- 1 cup mayonnaise
  Orange juice

Cut fish in ½-inch strips. Dip in flour, then in egg, then in bread crumbs; reserve. Peel and cut sweet potato into strips. Blanch in boiling water for 1 minute. Season with salt and pepper. Repeat procedure for fish. Cut bananas into strips and repeat procedure. Heat oil in skillet and fry first the sweet potato, then the bananas and finally the fish. Heap high on a warm platter. Keep warm.

Shred the orange and cook it in its own juice until pulpy. When cool, add to the mayonnaise. Add additional orange juice to taste. Pour sauce over potatoes, bananas and fish, and serve immediately.

Serves: 2

Wine: Montagny, Château de Davenay, Louis Latour 1967

Abbey Tavern
County Dublin, Ireland
Chef: William Marshall

SOLE ABBEY

4 1¼-pound (625-gram) Lambay or other
  available soles
½ cup Dublin Bay prawns or other large shrimp
½ teaspoon fennel seeds
½ teaspoon chopped chives
½ teaspoon chervil
½ cup chopped mushrooms
1 teaspoon chopped shallots
  Salt and freshly ground pepper to taste
½ cup dry white wine
½ cup fish stock
2 tablespoons chopped onion
1 bay leaf
1 teaspoon lemon juice
1 tablespoon catsup
1 tablespoon butter
2 tablespoons flour
4 tablespoons heavy cream
  Salt and freshly ground pepper to taste
2 cups Duchesse Potatoes (see index)
2 cups boiled, salted rice
½ head lettuce
8 tomato wedges
1 lemon, cut in wedges
  Cucumber slices
1 teaspoon chopped parsley

Fillet the soles into eight fillets. Combine prawns, fennel, chives, chervil and mushrooms to make a stuffing. Divide stuffing over fillets and roll each stuffed fillet separately. Secure with toothpicks.

Place shallots in a buttered pan and place rolled fillets on them. Season with salt and pepper, add white wine and enough stock to cover dish. Cover pan and poach slowly for 7 or 8 minutes with the chopped onion, bay leaf and lemon juice.

When cooked, remove fillets and keep hot. Reduce cooking liquid by about half. Color slightly with catsup. Combine butter and flour to make a roux and add to liquid to thicken to taste. Add cream and check seasonings.

Place half a circle of Duchesse Potatoes down one side of serving dish, and on the other side, the hot rice. Remove toothpicks and place sole in center. Cover with sauce. Garnish with lettuce leaves, wedges of tomato and lemon and slices of cucumber. Sprinkle with parsley.

Serves: 4

Carlton Tower Hotel

London, England

Chef: Bernard Gaume

SOLE CARLTON

2	shallots, chopped
1	cup butter
¾	cup chopped mushrooms
¾	cup Lobster Sauce (see index)
¾	cup cooked, chopped shrimp
1	teaspoon chopped chives
1	teaspoon finely chopped fennel
¾	cup heavy cream
	Salt and freshly ground pepper to taste
4	soles
	Salt and freshly ground pepper to taste
2	cups dry white wine
24	cooked green asparagus tips
1	teaspoon lemon juice

Toss 1 chopped shallot in ½ cup butter. Add mushrooms; as soon as they begin to dry, add Lobster Sauce. Reduce to desired consistency; then add chopped shrimp, chives and fennel. Stir in 3 tablespoons cream, season with salt and pepper and keep warm.

Remove the dark skin from the soles, cut off heads and clean white skin. Butter a heatproof dish; sprinkle the remaining chopped shallots on the bottom. Place soles in the dish, white skin on top, season, add the white wine, cover with buttered paper and cook for 30 minutes in a moderately slow (325° F.) oven. Remove soles and place on serving dish. Bone each fish. Stuff with the mushroom-Lobster Sauce mixture and reform the soles. Top with asparagus tips. Keep hot.

Reduce poaching liquid by half. Add the rest of the cream and continue reducing until thickened. Stir in remaining butter and lemon juice. Check seasoning and pour sauce over fish.

Serves: 4

Drouant

Paris, France

Chef: George Laffon

FILLETS OF SOLE DROUANT

2 1-pound (500-gram) soles
1 cup dry white wine
12 mussels in shells, scrubbed and trimmed
12 or more raw shrimp in shells
½ cup sliced mushrooms
½ cup butter
¼ cup chopped shallots
   Salt and freshly ground pepper to taste
1 cup heavy cream
1 clove garlic
3 tablespoons chopped parsley
1 tablespoon chopped fresh tarragon
3 tablespoons tomato paste
½ cup butter

Gut and trim the soles and cut them into fillets (be sure to remove all skin). Refrigerate until ready to cook. Make stock by simmering fish bones, 2 cups water and white wine together for 1 hour; strain. Simmer mussels in stock until they open and shrimp until shells turn pink. Remove and set aside. Sauté mushrooms very gently in butter until they are dry and dark brown.

Place shallots in a buttered baking dish. Arrange fillets of sole over shallots; dust with salt and pepper. Add 2 cups fish stock. Bake in a hot (400° F.) oven for about 10 minutes, or until fish flakes easily. Do not overcook.

Drain fillets carefully. To the stock, add the cream, garlic (on a toothpick, so that you can recover it when sauce is finished), parsley, tarragon and tomato paste. Reduce liquid to the consistency of very heavy cream. Stir in ½ cup butter.

To serve, place fillets on heatproof serving dish and arrange the mussels and shelled shrimp around sole; decorate with mushrooms. Spoon sauce over dish and glaze under the broiler (it will take only a minute or two). Serve very hot.

Serves: 4

Wine: Chablis "Fourchauine"

Restaurant Napoléon
Paris, France
Chef: Guy Baumann

SOLE POMPADOUR

```
 4  1-pound (500-gram) fillets of sole
¾  cup dry white wine
¾  cup fish stock
    Salt and freshly ground pepper to taste
 1  Bouquet Garni (see index)
12  shrimp
16  mussels
12  mushroom caps, sautéed in butter
¼  cup butter
¼  cup flour
 2  egg yolks
 6  tablespoons heavy cream
    Parsley sprigs
```

Poach fillets gently in white wine, fish stock, salt and pepper and Bouquet Garni for about 10 minutes. Cook and shell shrimp, leaving tails on. Reserve liquid. Steam and shell mussels, reserving liquid. Carefully place sole fillets on a service plate and arrange shrimp, mussels and mushrooms around fish.

Make a roux with the butter and flour; reduce cooking liquid from sole, mussels and shrimp to 2½ cups in all and add. Thicken with egg yolks and cream. Do not boil after eggs and cream have been added. To serve, pour over fish and decorate platter with parsley sprigs.

Serves: 4

Wine: Chablis

Hotel Gellèrt
Budapest, Hungary
Chef: Ferenc Novák

"BAKONY" FOGAS

(Fish Fillets with Mushroom Sauce)

```
 1  3-pound (1.5-kilogram) fogas or sole or
    other firm white-fleshed fish
 1  teaspoon salt
¼  cup finely chopped onion
¼  cup butter
 1  cup sliced mushrooms
½  teaspoon paprika
½  cup sour cream
¼  cup flour
 1  cup fish stock
    Salt to taste
 1  sprig parsley, chopped
 2  green peppers, cut into rings
```

Fillet the fish. Reserve head and all bones. Salt fillets and place in a buttered baking dish. Cook head and backbone in a small quantity of water. Brown onion in butter, add mushrooms and continue browning; sprinkle with paprika. Mix sour cream with flour and add with fish stock to mushrooms; bring to boil and salt slightly. Pour this mushroom sauce over fogas slices and bake in a moderate (350° F.) oven until tender. Sprinkle with chopped parsley before serving and garnish with green pepper rings. Serve with buttered noodles or potatoes if desired.

Serves: 4

Wine: Balatonfüred Rizling (white)

Malmaison Central Hotel
Glasgow, Scotland
Chef: J. M. Cottet

LA CASSEROLETTE DE FILETS DE SOLE DES MAITRES QUEUX

(Poached Sole in Pastry Shells)

12 large mushrooms
¼ cup chopped onion
1 clove garlic, finely chopped
¼ cup butter
4 sole fillets
2½ cups fish stock
½ cup Chablis
2½ cups heavy cream
2 egg yolks
2 tablespoons whipped cream
   Salt and freshly ground pepper to taste
   Butter
2 lobster claws, cooked and diced
1 cup puff pastry
4 sprigs parsley
4 slices truffle

Chop one half of the mushrooms, onion and garlic to prepare a duxelle. Cook in butter for 12 minutes; then put aside and keep warm.

Poach sole in fish stock and Chablis for 8 minutes. Remove fish from pan and keep warm. Reduce stock by two-thirds; add cream and reduce still further until sauce thickens. Remove from heat and stir in egg yolks. Quickly add whipped cream. Season the sauce and keep it warm.

Slice remaining mushrooms and sauté in butter; mix with diced lobster.

Make four large oval pastry cases from puff pastry and bake. Fill these with duxelle, fish, diced lobster and mushroom slices; cover with sauce. Glaze quickly under the broiler and garnish with parsley and truffle.

Serves: 4

Wine: Chablis

Quadri

Venice, Italy

Chef: Giovanni Mellina

FILETTI DI SOGLIOLA DELL'ADRIATICO ALLA BARCAROLA

(Adriatic Sole Fillets)

12 to 15 pieces of fillet of sole
   Salt to taste
   Flour
   Butter
¼ cup cognac
1½ cups mushrooms, sliced
¼ cup sherry
½ teaspoon fines herbes
1 cup heavy cream

Wash and thoroughly dry fillets. Salt and dredge in flour. Sauté in butter until they are lightly browned. Warm the cognac and pour over the fillets. Ignite. Add mushrooms and sherry. Shake the pan until the flames go out. Let simmer for 5 minutes. Then add fines herbes and cream. Cook until sauce is thickened. Serve on a very hot dish.

Serves: 4

Wine: Vino bianco secco (dry white wine)

Speilen, A/S Grand Hotel

Oslo, Norway

Chef: Nicòlo Castracaner

SOLE LAFAYETTE

1 tablespoon flour
1 tablespoon butter
1 teaspoon curry powder
⅓ cup dry white wine
⅓ cup Noilly Prat
6 sole fillets, cleaned
¼ cup chopped onion
¾ cup sliced mushrooms
¾ cup chopped tomatoes
1 bay leaf
   Thyme
   Salt and freshly ground pepper to taste
   Cayenne
½ cup butter
¼ cup sour cream
   Salt and freshly ground pepper to taste
1 teaspoon chopped parsley
1 tablespoon chopped watercress
¼ cup lemon juice

Knead flour and butter together to form beurre manié and add curry. Thicken white wine and Noilly Prat with this mixture and cook sole in it. Sauté onion, mushrooms, tomatoes and herbs and spices in butter until soft. Add the sour cream and 1 cup curry sauce from poaching fish. Season. Arrange sole on a silver dish and pour sauce over. Sprinkle with chopped parsley, watercress and lemon juice. Serve with boiled potatoes or rice pilaf, if desired.

Serves: 6

TOUR EIFFEL
Paris, France
Chef: Robert Saget
Duckling "Belle Epoque"
(page 52)

WHEELER'S
London, England
Chef: S. F. Chu
Oysters Mornay
(page 170)

RISTORANTE
"IL COCCODRILLO"
Florence, Italy
Chef: Francesco Dei
Fillet of Beef, Orloff's-style
(page 84)

WHEELER'S SOVEREIGN
London, England
Chef: Man Ying Sau
Moules à la Marinière
(page 171)

de Gravenmolen
Amsterdam, Netherlands
Chef: Alexander Koene

FILETS DE SOLE AUX FRUITS DE MER
(Poached Fillets of Sole with Shellfish in Lobster Sauce)

  1 **2-pound (1-kilogram) sole**
 ½ **cup fish stock**
  2 **peppercorns**
 ¼ **cup chopped shallots**
  1 **teaspoon lemon juice**
  2 **scampi**
  2 **lobster tails**
 12 **shrimp**
  6 **prawns**
  6 **mussels**
 1½ **tablespoons crab meat**
  2 **scallops**
  3 **pitted green olives**
  1 **tablespoon lobster butter**
 ¼ **cup brandy**
 ¼ **cup dry white wine**
  2 **cups lobster stock**
  2 **tablespoons flour**
  6 **tablespoons mushroom caps, browned in butter**
  1 **truffle, sliced**

Fillet sole and place in a large pan with fish stock, peppercorns, shallots, lemon juice, scampi, lobster tails, shrimp, prawns, mussels, crab meat, scallops, olives and lobster butter. Flame with brandy; add white wine and lobster stock. Poach gently until seafood is done, about 10 minutes. Do not overcook. Gently remove sole and shellfish to a serving platter. Strain the stock and thicken with flour. Cover seafood with sauce. Decorate platter with mushroom caps and truffle slices. Serve with Duchesse Potatoes (see index) and green salad, if desired.

Serves: 2

Wine: White Burgundy

Lorensberg Restaurant
Göteborg, Sweden
Chef: Allan Hult

CASSEROLETTE LORENSBERG

(Sole Tart)

Pie Shell

½ teaspoon salt
2 cups flour
1 cup butter

Sift salt with flour; cut butter into flour mixture. Add cold water a tablespoon at a time until dough holds its shape. Roll out to fit a 9-inch pan or tart dish. Bake in a very hot (450° F.) oven for about 10 minutes. Do not let crust get too brown.

Filling and Sauce

½ cup sliced mushrooms
½ cup butter
8 fillets of sole
1 cup dry white wine
1 cup heavy cream
1 tablespoon lobster butter
Salt to taste
1 tablespoon whiskey

Sauté mushrooms slightly in butter. Drain on absorbent paper. Fold sole fillets and poach in white wine and 1 cup water just until fish flakes easily. Gently remove fillets and reserve.

Reduce by half stock in which fish has been cooked; add cream and boil until thickened. Add lobster butter and season with salt. Finally, stir in a tablespoon of whiskey.

Conclusion

½ cup grated Gruyère cheese
½ cup cooked lobster meat

On bottom of the pie shell place sautéed and drained mushrooms, then poached fillets of sole. Fill shell with lobster sauce, and cover with grated cheese. Bake in a very hot (450° F.) oven until cheese melts and browns very lightly. Garnish with lobster meat.

Serves: 4

Wine: Chablis

Grand Hotel Royal
Stockholm, Sweden
Chef: Harry Westkamper

FRIED FILLET OF SOLE WITH CREAMED MUSHROOMS AND SHRIMP

 2 fillets of sole
 1 tablespoon flour
   Salt to taste
 1 teaspoon lemon juice
 1 teaspoon Worcestershire sauce
½ cup butter
½ cup cooked, shelled shrimp
½ cup chopped fresh dillweed
   Creamed Mushrooms (recipe follows)

Wash and dry fillets. Dredge in flour. Season with salt, lemon juice and Worcestershire sauce. Sauté fillets in butter about 8 minutes. Turn to brown evenly. Fish is done when it flakes easily; do not overcook. Cut fish into several smaller pieces. Reassemble fillets into original shape, using stuffing of Creamed Mushrooms to hold pieces together. Decorate with shrimp and chopped dillweed. Serve with boiled potatoes, if desired.

Creamed Mushrooms

1¼ cups sliced mushrooms
 ¼ cup butter
 1 teaspoon lemon juice
   Salt
1¼ cups heavy cream

Sauté mushrooms in butter about 5 minutes. Season with lemon juice and salt; stir in cream. Simmer gently to thicken.

Serves: 4

Auberge "Le Coeur Volant"
Louveciènnes, France
Chef: Bruno Belloni

TURBOT BRAISE AU CHAMPAGNE
(Braised Turbot with Champagne)

 4 turbot or sole fillets
 ¼ cup chopped shallots
 2 cups dry champagne
 1 cup heavy cream
   Bouquet Garni (see index)
   Dash cayenne
   Salt to taste
 ¼ cup butter
 4 small peeled tomatoes
12 cooked, shelled shrimp

Remove all skin from fish fillets and place in a buttered heatproof pan. Add shallots, 1½ cups champagne, cream, Bouquet Garni and seasonings. Cook in a moderate (350° F.) oven 10 minutes. Remove fillets and keep them warm on a serving dish. Boil down the sauce by about two-thirds. Add the remaining champagne and stir in butter. Check the seasoning and strain. Coat the fillets with sauce and arrange in a fan shape garnished with the tomatoes and shrimp.

Serves: 4

Wine: Chablis

Vinogradi
Belgrade, Yugoslavia
Chef: Živan Miljŭs

DANUBE FISH, SMEDEREVE-STYLE

¼ cup olive oil
1½ pounds (750 grams) trout or any other freshwater fish, boned
2½ cups chopped onions
2¼ cups mild, seeded, sliced green or red peppers
 1 small bunch celeriac, chopped
 2 bay leaves
2¼ cups boiled, sliced potatoes
 ½ teaspoon crushed garlic
   Paprika
   Salt and freshly ground pepper to taste
 ¼ cup dry white wine
 ¼ cup chopped parsley

Heat 2 tablespoons oil in skillet and sauté fish about 5 minutes on each side. Set aside. In a separate covered skillet, heat 2 tablespoons oil and sauté onion until soft. Add peppers, celeriac and bay leaves. Simmer, stirring, for 2 minutes until vegetables are coated with the oil. Add potatoes, garlic, paprika, salt and pepper and mix thoroughly. Add wine and parsley and simmer gently for 20 minutes until peppers are barely tender. Arrange the sautéed fish on a heatproof serving dish surrounded by vegetable mixture. Bake in a hot (450° F.) oven for 15 minutes. Serve very hot.

Serves: 4

Quaglino's
London, England
Chef: Peter Ferrero

TRUITE POCHEE EN VIN D'ALSACE

(Trout Poached in Alsatian Wine)

½ cup chopped shallots
¼ cup butter
 1 bay leaf
 4 ½-pound (250-gram) cleaned river trout
   Salt and freshly ground pepper to taste
1½ cups Alsatian hock or dry Riesling
 8 sautéed Fluted Mushrooms (see index)
 ½ cup fish velouté
 ¼ cup heavy cream
 ¼ cup chopped parsley
 8 fleurons

Very slowly cook chopped shallots with 2 tablespoons butter in a flameproof casserole. When tender, season trout with salt and pepper and add with bay leaf. Cover with wine and cook in a moderately hot (375° F.) oven for about 12 minutes. Remove trout from pan, skin and place on plate with mushrooms; keep warm until needed. Reduce stock by two-thirds; then add fish velouté and cream. Reduce again by half, remove from heat and finish with rest of butter. Correct seasoning. To serve trout, place two mushrooms on each, cover with sauce, sprinkle with chopped parsley and decorate with fleurons.

Serves: 4

Wine: Niersteiner Kranzberg 1967

F. Point, La Pyramide

Vienne, France

Chef: Guy Thivard

TRUITE FARCIE FERNAND POINT
(Stuffed Trout)

Stuffing

¼ cup diced carrots

¼ cup sliced mushrooms

¼ cup sliced truffles

¼ cup sliced white celery

2 tablespoons butter

2 tablespoons flour

2 egg yolks

Salt and freshly ground pepper to taste

Boil carrots gently in 1 cup lightly salted water for about 5 minutes. Drain. Combine with mushrooms, truffles and celery. Brown together in butter; then add flour. Remove from heat and stir in egg yolks. Mix thoroughly; cool. Season with salt and pepper.

Fish

2 ½-pound (250-gram) whole trout or other whitefish

2 tablespoons butter

½ cup sliced carrots

½ cup sliced onions

Thyme

1 cup port

3 tablespoons heavy cream

1 tablespoon flour

1 tablespoon butter

Gut, clean and bone the fish; fill it with mushroom-truffle stuffing and sew it up. Melt butter in a fish cooker or other heavy pan large enough not to crowd or break fish. Gently sauté carrots, onion and thyme for about 5 minutes. Carefully place fish in pan and add port. Cover with buttered paper or foil and place in a moderate (350° F.) oven for about ½ hour, or until fish flakes easily. Do not overcook.

When fish is cooked, place it on a serving dish and keep warm. Strain the sauce into a pan and add cream. Blend flour and butter and use to thicken sauce, if desired. Coat the fish with sauce and serve very hot.

Serves: 2

Wine: Gewurtztraminer

Seehaus
Zürich, Switzerland
Chef: H. Rudolph

TRUITE DU LAC SEEHAUS

(Trout from Lake Seehaus)

   1 2-pound (1-kilogram) trout
   1 cup dry white wine
   1 cup fish stock
   1 teaspoon butter
   3 tablespoons minced onion
   ¼ teaspoon minced parsley
   1½ tablespoons chopped tarragon
   ¼ teaspoon chopped dillweed
      Sauce (recipe follows)

Put the fish in buttered casserole with white wine, broth, butter, onion, parsley, tarragon and dillweed. Bake in a moderate (350° F.) oven for about 20 minutes, or until fish flakes easily. Do not overcook. Serve with sauce and boiled new potatoes, if desired.

Sauce

   1 cup heavy cream
   1 cup Hollandaise Sauce (see index)
   ½ teaspoon fines herbes
      Salt and freshly ground pepper to taste

Mix together cream, Hollandaise Sauce, fines herbes, salt and pepper. Chill.

Serves: 2 or 3

Wine: Riesling Sylvaner

Overton's
London, England
Chef: Carl Lerner

RIVER TROUT ST. JAMES

   6 small trout
   ½ cup milk
      Salt and freshly ground pepper to taste
   ¼ cup flour
   ¼ cup butter
   ½ pound (250 grams) shelled prawns or jumbo shrimp
   ½ lemon, seeded and peeled
   ½ pound (250 grams) smoked salmon
   1 cup diced mushrooms
   ¼ cup butter
   1 teaspoon Worcestershire sauce
   1 tablespoon chopped parsley

Clean trout and leave whole. Season milk with salt and pepper; dip trout in this mixture. Roll in flour and fry in butter for 8 to 10 minutes. Sauté prawns, lemon, smoked salmon and mushrooms in butter for 3 to 5 minutes with Worcestershire sauce. Pour over cooked trout and sprinkle with chopped parsley.

Serves: 6

Wine: Hock, Rhine, Liebfraumilch, Blue Nun

London Hilton

London, England

Chef: Oswald Mair

TRUITE SOUFFLE MONTGOLFIER

(Trout Soufflé)

8 small trout

2 cups Mouton Cadet white wine

1 teaspoon salt

1 tablespoon chopped tarragon

1 tablespoon chopped dillweed

Fish Forcemeat (recipe follows)

1 tablespoon finely chopped shallot

2½ cups fish stock

1¼ cups heavy cream

2 tablespoons butter

Slit trout down the back and remove bones. Wash, dry and marinate 30 minutes in 1 cup wine, salt and half the herbs. Fill each trout with about 3 tablespoons Fish Forcemeat and place in a large sauté pan. Add shallot, fish stock, marinade and remainder of wine. Poach gently for 8 to 10 minutes. Remove fish, take off skin and keep warm. Add the rest of the tarragon and dillweed to the cooking liquid and reduce by half. Adjust seasoning. Remove from heat and add cream. Beat in butter. Pour sauce over trout and serve immediately.

Fish Forcemeat

1 cup small pieces pike fillet

½ cup small pieces fillet of sole

½ cup small pieces turbot fillet

½ cup small pieces lobster meat

¼ cup Mouton Cadet white wine

½ teaspoon salt

½ teaspoon freshly ground pepper

10 tablespoons heavy cream

¼ cup strong fish stock

Salt and freshly ground pepper to taste

Marinate fish and lobster pieces in white wine with salt and pepper for 3 hours. Finely mince marinated fish and then rub through a fine sieve. Place in bowl, stir over crushed ice with a spatula until very smooth; add cream and fish stock a little at a time. When all is well mixed and smooth, season to taste.

Serves: 8

Wine: Mouton Cadet white

Esso Motor Hotel

Amsterdam, Netherlands

Chef: S. Tolsma

FILLET OF HALIBUT "LAFAYETTE"

Fillets

- 2 tablespoons butter
- 1 1¾-pound (875-gram) halibut, filleted
- ½ small leek, thinly sliced
- 1 teaspoon salt
- 1 bay leaf
- 1 sprig of parsley, chopped
- 4 slices lemon, peeled
- ⅓ cup dry white wine
- 2 medium sweet red peppers, chopped
- 2 medium sweet green peppers, chopped
- ½ cup sliced mushrooms

Grease a copper pan with the butter. Sauté filleted halibut lightly with leek, salt, bay leaf, parsley, lemon slices, white wine, red and green peppers and mushrooms. When fillets are lightly browned, cover the pan with foil and cook slowly until fish flakes easily, about 10 minutes.

Fennel Sauce

- ¼ cup dry white wine
- 2 tablespoons fennel vinegar
- 1 teaspoon salt
- 1 teaspoon freshly ground white pepper
- 1 bay leaf
- 1 tablespoon chopped onions
- 1 tablespoon fresh or dried fennel, or to taste
- 6 egg yolks
- ½ cup butter

Cook white wine, vinegar, salt, pepper, bay leaf, onion and fennel together until the mixture is quite thick and creamy. Sieve the mixture into a mixing bowl and beat in egg yolks thoroughly. Melt the butter and add it slowly to the sauce.

Conclusion

- 4 fleurons
- 4 sprigs parsley
- 1 lemon, quartered
  Chopped fennel

Place fillets and vegetables on warm dinner plates. Decorate each plate with a fleuron, a sprig of parsley, a lemon quarter and a sprinkling of chopped fennel. Pass sauce separately.

Serves: 4

Wine: Pouilly-Fuissé 1968

Hyde Park Hotel

London, England

Chef: Pierre Beaufort

TURBOT CITTOISE

(Turbot with Olives and Mushrooms)

1   5-pound (2.5-kilogram) turbot
6   large potatoes, peeled and quartered
½   cup sautéed potatoes
½   cup green olives, pitted
¼   cup button mushrooms, sautéed
½   cup lemon juice
2   cups browned butter

Split whole turbot down the center and fill pocket with potatoes. Sew up or skewer the pocket and bake in greased baking dish for 30 minutes in a hot (450° F.) oven. Remove fish from oven and place on serving dish. Remove potatoes from pocket; replace with sautéed potatoes, olives and button mushrooms. Dress with lemon juice and browned butter. Serve at once.

Serves: 6

Wine: Pouilly-Fumé 1967

Pierre

Pau, France

Chef: Roland Casau

LE SAUMON DU CAVE BRAISE AU JURANÇON

(Salmon Braised in White Wine)

½   cup chopped shallots
2   5-ounce (150-gram) center slices salmon
    Salt and freshly ground pepper to taste
⅔   cup dry white jurançon* or Chablis
2   cups fish stock
6   tablespoons heavy cream
¼   cup butter
    Jurançon

Butter a flameproof baking dish and cover the bottom of the dish with chopped shallots. Place salmon slices on shallots; dust with salt and pepper. Pour jurançon and fish stock over salmon and cover the dish with buttered parchment paper or foil. Bring the dish to a boil over direct heat; then place in a moderate (350° F.) oven. Remove from oven when center bone in the salmon gets loose, about 25 minutes. Remove bones and skin; arrange salmon slices in a serving dish. Reduce the cooking liquid by two-thirds, add cream, check the seasonings and bring to a boil again to blend. Mix in butter, beating until smooth with a wire whisk. Deglaze the baking dish with an additional tablespoon or two of wine and add to sauce.

Coat salmon slices with sauce and serve very hot.

Serves: 2

*Jurançon is a French dry white country wine.

Wärdshuset Stallmästaregården

Stockholm, Sweden

Chef: Walter Wirz

CHARCOAL-BROILED DILL-CURED SALMON WITH MUSTARD SAUCE

4 pounds (2 kilograms) salmon, center cut

2 tablespoons coarse salt

2 tablespoons sugar

1 tablespoon crushed white peppercorns

½ cup coarsely chopped dillweed

Butter

Dill sprigs

Mustard Sauce (recipe follows)

Wipe salmon but do not rinse. Remove backbone and side bones and cut into two pieces lengthwise. Rub inside of salmon with coarse salt, sugar and crushed white peppercorns. Place one piece of salmon, skin side down, in a pan or bowl just large enough to hold it. Cover with one-third of chopped dillweed. Place the second piece of salmon on top, skin side up, so that the thicker portion of the fish rests on the thinner part of the bottom piece. Cover with weighted plate and refrigerate for 24 hours. Turn fish over twice during this period and add more dillweed. Wipe off spices and dillweed and remove; reserve salmon skin. Cut salmon into thick slices. Broil each piece on charcoal grill (or under the broiler) until fish flakes easily. While fish cooks, cut skin into ½-inch strips and sear in butter. Garnish grilled slices with fresh dill sprigs and crisp salmon skin. Serve with Mustard Sauce.

Mustard Sauce

1 tablespoon mild mustard

1 teaspoon dark French mustard

1 teaspoon sugar

1 tablespoon wine vinegar

Pinch of salt

¼ teaspoon freshly ground white pepper

1 teaspoon lemon juice

3 tablespoons salad oil (not olive oil)

3 tablespoons finely chopped dillweed

Combine mustards, sugar, vinegar, salt, pepper and lemon juice. Blend well. Add oil, a few drops at a time, beating constantly to make a smooth mayonnaiselike sauce. Stir in finely chopped dillweed. Serve at room temperature. Store extra sauce tightly covered in the refrigerator.

Serves: 6

Wine: White Bordeaux

Aurora

Stockholm, Sweden

Chef: Staffan Enander

MARINATED SALMON FROM THE CHARCOAL GRILL

- 1 **5-pound (2.5-kilogram) boneless fillet of salmon**
- ¾ **cup sugar**
- 6 **tablespoons salt**
- 1 **tablespoon crushed white peppercorns**
- 1 **cup coarsely chopped dillweed**
  Oil
  Sweet Mustard Sauce (recipe follows)

Wipe salmon with a damp cloth and dry well. Do not hold under water. Marinate the fillets in a dry mixture of sugar, salt, white pepper and the dillweed for 6 hours at room temperature and then 18 in the refrigerator. With knife held at an angle, cut salmon into ¼-pound skinless slices. Keep skin as intact as possible. Cut skin into inch-wide strips, oil lightly and grill quickly with the salmon over charcoal. Serve some crisp skin with each fillet. Accompany with Sweet Mustard Sauce.

Sweet Mustard Sauce

- 2 **cups sweet mustard**
- 4 **cups oil**
- ¾ **cup sugar**
- 1 **tablespoon vinegar**
- 1 **teaspoon salt**
- 1 **teaspoon freshly ground white pepper**

Mix all ingredients thoroughly. Store any extra sauce tightly covered in the refrigerator.

Serves: 20 as a first course or 6 as a main dish

Wine: Dry white wine, beer or schnapps

Ostermalmskällaren

Stockholm, Sweden

Chef: Jacques Debin

SALMON PASTRY

  1 **3-pound (1.5-kilogram) salmon**
  1 **2-pound (1-kilogram) pike**
     Salt and freshly ground pepper to taste
  4 **egg whites**
1¼ **cups heavy cream**
  ½ **cup Lobster Sauce (see index)**
  ¼ **cup cognac**
  ¼ **cup dry white wine**
  1 **cup pâte à chou**
  ½ **cup sliced mushrooms**
  ½ **cup cooked, shelled shrimp**
     Green Mayonnaise (recipe follows)

Bone the fish. Reserve some slices of salmon; pass the rest of the salmon and pike flesh through the mincer twice. Keep the minced fish cool, add salt and pepper and mix well. Stir in the egg whites, cream, Lobster Sauce, cognac, wine and pâte à chou. Fill a large pastry tin with layers of fish mixture, the mushrooms, then shrimp and salmon slices. Cook for about 1½ hours in a moderate (350° F.) oven. Chill, slice and serve with Green Mayonnaise.

Green Mayonnaise

  ½ **cup watercress**
  ½ **cup raw spinach**
  ¼ **cup fresh tarragon or chervil**
  ¼ **cup chopped onion**
  2 **teaspoons lemon juice**
  1 **cup thick mayonnaise**

Scald greens in boiling water. Drain. Pound with onion and lemon juice in mortar or liquefy in electric blender. Add essence of greens to mayonnaise and mix well.

Serves: 25

Wine: White Burgundy

Savoy Hotel
Malmö, Sweden
Chef: Einar Petersson

LOX A LA SAVOY

1 cup spinach
4 hard-cooked eggs
8 slices raw marinated salmon
   Gyllenhammar Potatoes (recipe follows)

Cook spinach. Drain well. Chop eggs and mix with spinach. Spread mixture on the salmon slices. Place each slice on a piece of greaseproof paper and fold up paper into individual packets. Place packets of salmon in a hot (450° F.) oven for about 10 minutes. Serve on a warm plate, having first cut away paper with scissors. Serve with Gyllenhammar Potatoes.

Gyllenhammar Potatoes

2 cups cubed raw potatoes
½ cup butter
1¼ cups heavy cream
1½ tablespoons salt
   Freshly ground pepper to taste
1 tablespoon chopped parsley

Lightly and quickly sauté potatoes in butter. Add cream, salt and pepper; simmer until potatoes are tender. Sprinkle with chopped parsley.

Serves: 4

Wine: Traminer Schlossberg

Castillane
Birmingham, England
Chef: Allan Mackie

FRESH AND SMOKED SALMON PATE MOUSSE

¼ cup finely chopped onions
   Butter
1½ cups raw fresh salmon, filleted
½ cup smoked salmon, boned and skinned
½ cup pieces of filleted halibut
   Salt and freshly ground pepper to taste
3¾ cups heavy cream
3 tablespoons dry vermouth
10 miniature smoked salmon cornets
1 small tomato rose
1 cup clear aspic, melted

Lightly sauté onion in butter; do not brown. Pass all fish through fine blade of food chopper with onion. Add seasoning. Force all through fine-mesh wire sieve. Put into a medium-sized mixing bowl. Slowly incorporate cream into fish mixture with a wooden spoon. Add wine in the same way. Check seasoning. Pour into a soufflé dish, filling to the top. Place dish in a pan containing ½ inch boiling water. Bake, covered, in a moderately slow (325° F.) oven for 1½ hours. Cool and then chill. Turn out on a serving plate. Garnish with miniature cornets and tomato rose glazed in aspic.

Serves: 10

Wine: Sancerre

A l'Ecu de France
London, England
Chef: J. Pedri

SALMON KOULIBIAC

Brioche Dough

    3 eggs
    1 tablespoon dried yeast or 1 cake fresh yeast
    1 teaspoon sugar
    2 cups flour
 1½ teaspoons salt
    2 teaspoons sugar
    ¾ cup unsalted butter, chilled

Start brioche dough early on the day you will need it (or make it the day before and refrigerate overnight). Have eggs at room temperature. Beat them slightly, just enough to break up. Dissolve yeast in 3 tablespoons lukewarm water with 1 teaspoon sugar.

Sift flour, salt and 2 teaspoons sugar together. Make a well in the center and add eggs and completely dissolved yeast. Stir to mix all ingredients thoroughly. The dough will be very sticky and soft. Turn dough out on a board. Work with a spatula or two knives to finish mixing and form dough into a ball. Let rest.

Working quickly, mash chilled butter into small flat pieces. The pieces should be flexible but not melted.

Knead dough until it begins to hold together. Flour board as necessary. Add butter, a few bits at a time, kneading and cutting dough. Refrigerate dough and butter if the butter starts to melt.

When all the butter is incorporated and dough looks fluffy, let it rest for 5 minutes. Then knead a few more turns and place in a large bowl. Cover with plastic film and let rise until triple in volume. Punch down and knead thoroughly. Let rise again until double in volume. Punch down and knead lightly. Chill for 30 minutes, or until you are ready to use.

Filling

 2½ ounces dried vesiga (dried sturgeon marrow)
     Chicken consommé or water
    3 cups salmon pieces
    1 cup butter
    ½ cup sliced mushrooms
    1 tablespoon chopped onion
    1 cup cracked wheat (semolina kache)
 2½ cups chicken consommé
    2 hard-cooked eggs, chopped
    ½ cup melted butter

Soak the dried vesiga, which is in powder form, for at least 4 hours in cold water to cover and then cook for 3½ hours in consommé or water. This will yield 2 cups cooked vesiga. Sauté salmon pieces briefly in 1 cup butter. Set aside. Sauté mushrooms and chopped onion in butter. Cook cracked wheat in consommé. Mix with chopped eggs and cooked vesiga.

Conclusion

Roll the brioche dough into two rectangles 12 inches long by 8 inches wide. Spread with layers of cooked cracked wheat, salmon, chopped vesiga-egg mixture and mushrooms and onion. Finish with a layer of cooked cracked wheat. Moisten edges of dough and draw over stuffing to form

12- by 4-inch rectangles. Seal the dough on all sides. Place the two koulibiac on baking tray, taking care that seams in the dough lie on the bottom. Let dough rise for 25 minutes. Sprinkle koulibiac with ½ cup melted butter. Make a small slit on top of each to allow steam to escape.

Preheat oven to very hot (475° F.). Bake the koulibiac for 15 to 20 minutes. When raised and lightly brown, reduce heat to moderate (350° F.). Total baking time should be about 45 to 50 minutes. Pour freshly melted butter into koulibiac through slit in top after taking from oven.

Serves: 10

Wine: Chevalier-Montrachet, Domaine Lefla 1966

Prestonfield House Hotel
Edinburgh, Scotland
Chef: Franck Fusco

SMOKED HADDOCK MOUSSE

2 tablespoons unflavored gelatin
¼ cup sliced stuffed green olives
¼ cup sliced ripe olives
1 pound smoked haddock
1¼ cup milk
   Mixed herbs (tarragon, dill, etc.)
2 tablespoons butter
2 tablespoons flour
1 egg, beaten
1¼ cups heavy cream
   Lemon juice
   Freshly ground pepper to taste

Dissolve gelatin in 1¼ cups hot water. When cool, use some of it to line individual molds or one large mold. Decorate the bottom with slices of green and ripe olives held in place with a little more aspic jelly. Refrigerate molds until required.

Poach haddock in milk with mixed herbs for 6 to 10 minutes. When done, strain off milk and reserve it for the sauce. Remove skin and bones from fish and flake the flesh finely. Make a roux of the butter and flour; cook, stirring, for 5 minutes. Then add the milk in which fish was cooked. When sauce has cooled, add rest of aspic jelly, fish, egg, cream, lemon juice and pepper. Fill molds with this mixture and refrigerate until set (several hours). Turn out before serving.

Serves: 6 to 8

Wine: Chablis

The Russell

Dublin, Ireland

Chef: Jackie Needham

SAUMON FROID EN BELLE VUE
(Cold Salmon)

 1 10-pound (5-kilogram) salmon
 1 cup sliced carrots
 4 medium onions
 1 tablespoon peppercorns
 ½ cup sliced pitted black olives
 2 peeled tomatoes, cut in wedges and seeded
 2 leeks
 1 dozen cooked, shelled prawns or jumbo shrimp
  Aspic (recipe follows)
 2 long loaves unsliced bread
 4 tablespoons softened butter
  Duchesse Potatoes (recipe follows)
  Herb Juice (recipe follows)

Cook salmon with carrots, onions and peppercorns in salted water barely to cover. When done, allow to cool; then remove from pan. Reserve stock. Skin salmon, cover with a damp cloth and place in the refrigerator to chill. When fish is completely cold, decorate with black olive slices, tomato wedges, the green part of the leeks and the prawns. Glaze with aspic and refrigerate until set.

To serve, remove crusts from loaves of bread and arrange on a silver dish. Spread bread with softened butter. Place decorated salmon on bread and pipe Duchesse Potatoes tinted green with Herb Juice all around platter decoratively. Serve with mayonnaise or Sauce Verte.

Aspic

 3 pounds (1.5 kilograms) sole bones
  Stock from poaching salmon
 ½ teaspoon thyme
 2 sprigs parsley
 1 bay leaf
 2 cups chopped whiting
 6 egg whites
  Salt and freshly ground pepper to taste
 2 tablespoons unflavored gelatin

Boil bones, stock, additional water to cover, if necessary, thyme, parsley and bay leaf together for 15 minutes. Strain into a saucepan; add whiting and egg whites. Bring to a boil; then simmer until stock is clear. Strain. Season with salt and pepper. Soften gelatin in ¼ cup cold water and add. Allow to cool to consistency of egg whites before using to glaze salmon.

Duchesse Potatoes

- **2 pounds (1 kilogram) potatoes, peeled**
- **2 tablespoons butter**
  Salt and freshly ground pepper to taste
- **3 egg yolks**

Cook potatoes; mash and add butter, salt, pepper and egg yolks. Beat well.

Herb Juice

- **2 tablespoons chopped parsley**
- **2 tablespoons chopped chervil**
- **2 tablespoons chopped tarragon**
- **2 tablespoons chopped chives**
- **2 tablespoons chopped spinach**
- **2 tablespoons chopped watercress**

Scald all greens in boiling water for 2 minutes. Immediately plunge into cold water. Pound in a mortar and strain juice, or liquefy in an electric blender. Use to color Duchesse Potatoes and to make Sauce Verte (¼ cup herb juice mixed with 1 cup mayonnaise).

Serves: 4 to 6

Wine: Corton-Charlemagne 1966

National Hotel

Moscow, Soviet Union

STURGEON A LA MOSCOW

- **4 sturgeon fillets***
- **1 egg**
- **2 tablespoons flour**
- **2 tablespoons butter**
- **½ cup grated mild hard cheese**

Pat fillets dry with paper towels. Beat egg with 1 teaspoon cold water. Dredge fillets in flour; then dip in egg mixture. Sauté in butter over medium heat until fillets are golden on both sides. Remove from pan and sprinkle with grated cheese. Boiled potatoes (with more butter) are traditionally served with sturgeon.

Serves: 2

*If sturgeon is not available, sole, flounder or shad may be substituted, but of course the experience will not be exactly like eating Sturgeon à la Moscow.

Grand Hotel Margitsziget
Budapest, Hungary
Chef: Bálint Miklós

JELLIED CARP, HUNGARIAN-STYLE

  1 1¾-pound (875-gram) carp
     Salt to taste
  2 sets roe
  1 cup milk
  1 cup chopped onion
  1 green pepper, finely chopped
  2 tomatoes, peeled and seeded
  ½ teaspoon paprika
  1 tablespoon unflavored gelatin
  2 egg whites
  2 hard-cooked eggs, sliced
  1 canned pimiento, drained and slivered
     Salad greens
  1 lemon, cut in wedges

Skin fish, remove bones and fillet. Wash and salt fillets and put aside. Wash and salt roes and put to soak in milk. Cook the onion, half the green pepper and the tomato over low heat, stirring often to avoid burning. Poach the carp with the roes in the milk just until fillets flake and roe is set. Do not overcook. Remove fish and roes from broth; cool. Add paprika and gelatin to the broth and clarify it with egg whites. Arrange cool fish fillets and roes in a deep dish, decorate with slices of egg, the remaining green pepper and the pimiento. Cover with the clear broth and refrigerate until set (several hours or overnight). Unmold on serving plate decorated with salad greens and serve with lemon wedges.

Serves: 5

Wine: Chablis

Nandron
Lyon, France
Chef: ID

QUENELLES DE BROCHET "NANDRON"

(Pike Quenelles)

  1 4-pound (2-kilogram) pike
  2 cups heavy cream
     Salt to taste
     Cayenne
  4 eggs

Cut pike into fillets. Strain the flesh into a mixing bowl through a fine sieve. Set the bowl in a larger vessel filled with cracked ice. Beat in cream slowly. Add salt, cayenne and eggs. Mix in carefully.

Let mixture rest in the refrigerator for 24 hours. Roll the quenelles to the desired size on a cold floured marble surface. Poach in water just below the boiling point; then put in cold water. These quenelles go well with Sauce à la Lyonnaise, Nantua or Financière, if desired.

Serves: 6

Wine: Chante-Alouette

Bristol

Warsaw, Poland

KARP PO POLSKU

(Carp Polonaise)

- 1 4-pound (2-kilogram) cleaned carp
- 1 tablespoon salt
- 2½ cups julienne mixed vegetables (carrots, onions, leeks, parsnips, etc.)
- ¼ teaspoon freshly ground pepper
- ¼ cup lemon juice
- ¼ cup dry white wine
  Sauce (recipe follows)

Cut the fish into serving portions and salt. Poach the carp with vegetables, adding pepper, lemon juice and white wine.

Arrange fish on serving platter with boiled potatoes, if desired. Pour sauce over all and pass extra sauce separately.

Sauce

- 2¼ cups honeycomb
- 1 cup and 2 tablespoons raisins
- 1 cup and 2 tablespoons blanched almonds
- 1¼ cups butter
- ⅓ cup flour
- 4 cups consommé
- 1 tablespoon cinnamon
- ¼ teaspoon ground cloves
- 1 cup honey
- 1 cup lemon juice
- 1 cup orange juice
- 1 cup Madeira
  Sugar

Soak the honeycomb in hot water; soak raisins and almonds separately. Make a roux of the butter and flour; stir in consommé, cinnamon, cloves, squeezed honeycomb and honey. Mix the components and rub through a sieve, add lemon and orange juices, Madeira, raisins and almonds. Season with sugar to taste.

Serves: 4

Wine: Chablis

Kalastajatorppa

Helsinki, Finland

Chef: Kalervo Paakkinen

BURBOT PASTY CABANE

(Cod Liver Pasty)

1¼ cups cooked, sliced burbot (cod) liver
2 cups flaky pastry
1 cup boiled rice
6 hard-cooked eggs, sliced
1½ pounds (750 grams) burbot, chopped
½ cup chopped dillweed
    Salt and freshly ground pepper to taste
1 egg yolk, lightly beaten
    Sauce (recipe follows)

Wash liver in salted water. In a covered saucepan, simmer liver in water to cover for about 15 minutes. Drain. Slice and set aside.

Roll out flaky pastry to ¼-inch thickness and cut out two fish-shaped pieces. Place one pastry piece in heatproof serving dish. In alternating layers, place rice, sliced eggs, burbot and burbot liver. Sprinkle on dillweed and season with salt and pepper. Fit other pastry piece on top and press edges together. Glaze with egg yolk. Bake in a hot (400° F.) oven for 45 minutes. Serve with sauce.

Sauce

¾ cup dry white wine
¼ cup finely chopped onion
6 egg yolks
1¾ cups butter, melted
¾ cup heavy cream, boiling
    Salt and freshly ground pepper to taste

In a saucepan, bring wine to boil and add onion. Boil for about 5 minutes. Remove from heat and beat in the egg yolks until sauce is creamy and thick enough to coat a spoon. Return to heat, add melted butter and stir well. Pour in cream, stirring constantly. Season to taste with salt and pepper.

Serves: 4

Wine: Chablis

Nandron

Lyon, France

Chef: ID

SUPREME DE TURBOT AU VIN DE POUILLY

(Turbot Fillet with Wine)

4 ½-pound (250-gram) turbot fillets
  Salt to taste
  Cayenne
1 cup cooked, flaked pike
½ cup crushed, sieved tomatoes
½ cup butter, melted
½ cup chopped mushrooms
  Dash paprika
¾ cup heavy cream, whipped
  Salt to taste
1 cup fish stock
½ cup very dry Pouilly-Fuissé

1 cup sole stock
1 tablespoon flour
2 tablespoons Hollandaise Sauce (see index)
½ cup crayfish claws
½ cup sliced truffles

Cut the turbot into fillets; slice each fillet into four portions. Season well with salt and cayenne.

In the meantime, prepare a mousse of pike. Mix flaked pike with tomatoes, butter, mushrooms and paprika. Blend well. Fold in whipped cream. Add salt. Chill until very thick.

On each of four 8- by 10-inch sheets of buttered cooking parchment, spread a tablespoon of mousse; top with four portions of the turbot fillet. Coat well with the mousse and fold, pressing lightly to obtain a rectangle. Secure paper with skewers or string. Poach for 20 minutes in fish stock to which wine has been added.

Lightly thicken sole stock with flour. Add Hollandaise Sauce to obtain a medium thick sauce. Remove the fillets from the paper; arrange on a plate; pour the sauce over them. Garnish with crayfish and truffle slices and serve very hot.

Serves: 4

Wine: Pouilly-Fuissé

Carpati

Brasov, Romania

Chef: Ion Dosu

DELIGHT OF ZANDER

¾ cup butter

1 cup flour

4 teaspoons salt

2 pounds (1 kilogram) zander (perch pike) fillets

¼ cup dry white wine

1 cup chopped onions

1 cup sliced mushrooms
  Pinch freshly ground pepper

1 cup chopped tomatoes

1 egg yolk, lightly beaten

1 cup heavy cream

¼ cup lemon juice

Prepare the dough by blending ½ cup butter, ¾ cup flour and 2 teaspoons salt. Set aside.

Poach fillets in wine, onion, mushrooms, 2 teaspoons salt and pinch of pepper for 15 minutes. Add chopped tomatoes and continue to poach for another 15 minutes. Meanwhile, roll out dough on floured board to about ½-inch thickness. Cut in crescent shapes, place on a cookie sheet and glaze with egg yolk. Bake in a very hot (450° F.) oven for 15 minutes, or until pastry is golden brown.

While pastry is baking, remove fillets from their cooking liquid and keep hot on a serving dish. Thoroughly blend ¼ cup flour into the stock. Gradually add the cream, stirring constantly until well blended. Stir in ¼ cup butter about a teaspoon at a time until thoroughly mixed. Finally, stir in the lemon juice and simmer until sauce is creamy and thick enough to coat a spoon. Strain. Pour sauce over the fillets and arrange pastry crescents around them. Serve immediately.

Serves: 4

Chez Puget (Le Petit Brouant)

Nice, France

Chef: Gaston Puget

ROUGETS EN CAISSETTE

(Red Mullet in Paper Pockets)

    Salad oil
24 small mullet
 1 cup Bread Stuffing (recipe follows)
 1 cup sliced mushrooms
 1 cup cooked mussels
 8 mushroom caps
16 truffle slices
¼ cup buttered bread crumbs

Prepare eight cooking parchment pockets. Oil lightly with salad oil. Skin mullet. Place a layer of stuffing in each parchment pocket. Arrange three mullet, slices of mushrooms and a few mussels in each one. Top with stuffing, mushroom caps and two slices of truffle. Sprinkle with bread crumbs and secure pockets with skewers or string. Bake in a shallow pan in a moderately hot (375° F.) oven for about 20 minutes. Fish is done when it flakes easily. Do not overcook.

Bread Stuffing

¾ cup coarse bread crumbs
¼ cup minced onion
¼ cup minced celery
 2 tablespoons minced parsley
 1 teaspoon sage
½ teaspoon thyme
   Salt and freshly ground pepper to taste
 1 egg, beaten
½ cup fish stock or chicken broth

Mix all ingredients, adding stock a little at a time to make a thick paste. Extra stuffing can be baked separately in a hot (400° F.) oven for 10 to 15 minutes.

Serves: 8

Wine: Blanc che Bellit

The Empress

London, England

Chef: G. Scandolo

TURBOT A LA FACON DU CHEF
(Chef's Special Turbot)

    2 pounds (1 kilogram) fresh whiting fillets
      Salt and freshly ground pepper to taste
    3 egg whites
2½ cups heavy cream
    1 6-pound (3-kilogram) turbot
    ¼ cup sliced onion
    1 bay leaf
    ¼ cup minced parsley
      Salt and freshly ground pepper to taste
    ½ cup Chablis
1½ cups sliced mushrooms
1¼ cups fish stock
    2 tablespoons butter
      Lobster Sauce (recipe follows)

Dry whiting fillets in a cloth and pass through a fine mincer twice. Place in a cold mixing bowl, add seasoning and blend. Put the bowl on ice; add egg whites, one at a time, using a wooden spoon. Add cream very slowly, taking care that all ingredients are mixed to a thick creamy consistency.

Remove central bone from turbot and fill resulting cavity with whiting mixture. Place in large pan and add onion, bay leaf, parsley, salt, pepper, Chablis, mushrooms, fish stock and butter. Cover with foil and cook in a moderate (350° F.) oven for about 1 hour. Remove black skin and side bones from turbot. Place on serving dish and arrange cooked mushrooms around fish. Add Lobster Sauce to the cooking liquor. Reduce mixture by half and pass through a fine strainer. Coat turbot with sauce and serve remainder from sauceboat.

Lobster Sauce

      Shell from at least 1 cooked lobster
      Butter
    ⅓ cup flour
    ⅓ cup butter
1½ cups lobster stock or light consommé
    1 cup heavy cream
      Leftover lobster meat (if available), diced
      Salt and freshly ground pepper to taste

Crush shells (as many as possible) with a mallet. Heat very slowly with butter for 1 hour. Strain butter—discard shells.

Blend flour and butter together to make a roux. Cook over low heat for 5 minutes. Add stock and cream. Cook, but do not boil, until sauce thickens. Add diced lobster meat and salt and pepper to taste.

Serves: 8 to 10

Wine: Beaune "Clos des Mouches" Joseph Drouin 1966

Maison Prunier
London, England
Chef: Jean Lecorre

PATE DE POISSON TRAKTIR
(Fish Pâté)

2 pounds (1 kilogram) filleted turbot or cod
¼ cup dry white wine
2 tablespoons whiskey
½ teaspoon thyme
1 bay leaf
½ teaspoon salt
½ teaspoon freshly ground pepper
1 cup seasoned bread crumbs
1 cup heavy cream
1 cup chopped mushrooms
½ cup cooked sorrel,* drained and minced
½ cup chopped shallots
1 teaspoon minced savory
1 teaspoon minced chervil
  Salt and freshly ground pepper to taste
12 thin pancakes (see "Crêpes" in index)

Marinate half the fish fillets in wine, whiskey, thyme, bay leaf, salt and pepper for 2 hours. Then simmer in marinade for 5 or 6 minutes, or just until fish flakes easily; do not overcook.

Mince the other half of the fish very finely in a food mill. Add to it bread crumbs and cream. Mix thoroughly.

Sauté chopped mushrooms, sorrel, shallots, savory, chervil, salt and pepper until all mushroom liquid is evaporated and mixture is very dark. Mix with one-third of the minced fish mixture and reserve.

Butter a 2-quart heatproof dish. Line with thin pancakes. Spread a layer of minced-fish–crumb mixture on the bottom. Then arrange a layer of poached fillets on stuffing. Top with a layer of the mushroom mixture. Repeat until mold is full.

Cook in a bath of simmering water in a moderately slow (325° F.) oven for 30 minutes. Remove, press out and drain off any liquid that has accumulated. Cover with a plate and weigh down slightly. Chill overnight; then unmold on a serving platter.

Serves: 12

*If not available, ½ cup cooked spinach and 2 teaspoons lemon juice may be substituted.

Wine: Chablis le Cru Fourchaume 1967

Le Nord

Lyon, France

Chef: Claude Ovise

LA MATELOTE D'ANGUILLES A LA LYONNAISE

(Eel Stew)

    2 pounds (1 kilogram) eels, with fins and
      heads
    ½ cup butter
    2 tablespoons cognac
    1 cup larding bacon
    ¾ cup diced carrots
    ½ cup diced onions
    1 sprig thyme
    ½ bay leaf
    1 sprig parsley
    3 cups Beaujolais
    1 cup Pouilly-Fuissé
      Salt and freshly ground pepper to taste
      Fried bread slices

Cut heads and tails off eels and reserve. Cut remaining eel flesh into pieces, brown in butter and flame in cognac. Reserve. Brown the heads and fins of the eels with pieces of larding bacon, carrots, onions, thyme, bay leaf and parsley. Add Beaujolais and Pouilly-Fuissé and let this stock simmer for 3 hours. Extract the eel heads and crush through a fine sieve. Add purée to stock. When liquid starts to boil, add the eel. Place in a moderately slow oven, covered, to heat through. Correct the seasoning. Add butter, if desired; serve with fried bread.

Serves: 6

Wine: Pouilly-Fuissé blanc

Fim do Mundo

Cascais, Portugal

Chef: Antonio Cerdeira

CALDEIRADA

(Fish Stew)

    4 slices hake
    3 medium onions, thinly sliced
    3 medium tomatoes, chopped
    3 tablespoons olive oil
      Salt to taste
    1 small live lobster, cooked and shelled
    2 cups cooked, shelled prawns
    2 cups cooked, shelled shrimp
    2 cups clams in shells
    1 cup cooked green peas
      Chili peppers, according to taste

Scald hake in boiling water and place in bottom of earthenware pot. Sauté onion and tomatoes in olive oil, seasoned with salt. Cover hake with this mixture. Simmer over low heat until hake is cooked.

Cut lobster in slices and add. Add the prawns, shrimp, clams, peas and chili peppers. Cover pot and cook until clam shells open.

Serves: 4

Wine: Vinho Verde Alvarinho

Varanda do Chanceler
Lisbon, Portugal
Chef: Celso Balado Alvarez

MARISCOS NA POCA
(Seafood Chowder)

¼ cup chopped onions
¼ cup chopped leeks
2 garlic cloves, chopped
1 bay leaf
1 tablespoon butter
½ cup chopped tomatoes
5 cups fish broth
Salt to taste
6 sprigs mint
1¼ cups shelled shrimp
1¼ cups lobster meat
1¼ cup shelled crayfish
1¼ cups shelled clams
1 cup heavy cream
Fried bread slices

Simmer onion, leek, garlic and bay leaf in butter and ½ cup water. Add tomatoes, fish broth seasoned with salt and a few mint leaves. Bring to a boil and simmer for 15 minutes. Strain through a sieve and add shrimp, lobster meat, crayfish, clams and cream. Cook until tender. Serve very hot on slices of fried bread, garnished with a sprig of mint.

Serves: 2 or 3

London Hilton
London, England
Chef: Oswald Mair

LES TROIS COQUILLES DE FRUITS DE MER
(Coquilles of Seafood)

1 cup leaf spinach
12 scallop shells
4 pieces filleted sole, poached
1 cup cooked, buttered rice
2½ cups curried large prawns or jumbo shrimp
1 cup stewed tomatoes
2 cups cooked lobster meat
½ cup rich white sauce
2 tablespoons sherry
2 cups Duchesse Potatoes (see index)
2 cups Hollandaise Sauce (see index)

Cook spinach and drain very thoroughly. Cover bottom of four scallop shells with spinach and place one piece of sole in each. Cover bottom of next four shells with buttered rice and top with curried prawns. Cover bottom of last four shells with stewed tomatoes and top with lobster meat moistened with white sauce and sherry (à la Newburg). Place all shells on a heatproof platter, cover each one with Hollandaise Sauce and decorate rim of scallop shells with a piping of Duchesse Potatoes. Glaze to golden brown under the broiler.

Serves: 4

Wine: Champagne

Gambrinus

Lisbon, Portugal

PARRICHADA DE MARISCOS
(Broiled Seafood)

1 1½-pound (750-gram) live lobster
1 tablespoon olive oil
4 crayfish
4 prawns
8 shrimp
4 oysters
4 mussels
8 clams
½ cup melted butter
   Salt to taste
   Juice of ½ lemon
¼ teaspoon hot pepper sauce

Split lobster lengthwise; clean, sprinkle with olive oil and broil 10 minutes. Add crayfish, prawns, shrimp and, lastly, oysters, mussels and clams on the half-shell. Arrange seafood attractively on dish and serve with hot melted butter seasoned with salt, lemon juice and a few drops of hot pepper sauce.

Serves: 4

The Caprice

London, England

Chef: Brian Cotterill

HOMARD A LA PARISIENNE
(Lobster in Aspic)

1 6-pound (3-kilogram) live lobster
2 tablespoons sliced truffles
2 cups clear aspic
   Salad greens
4 stuffed egg halves
½ cup peeled, sliced cucumber
12 cherry tomatoes
½ cup mayonnaise

Cook lobster and remove meat. Cut into slices, decorate with pieces of truffle and glaze with part of aspic. Arrange lobster shell on an oval dish lined with more aspic. The claws should be pointing upward and the emptied shell should be on its back. Arrange lobster slices around shell. Cover dish with remaining aspic and chill until set. Unmold on a bed of salad greens and garnish with stuffed egg halves, cucumber slices and cherry tomatoes. Serve with mayonnaise.

Serves: 4

Wine: Corton-Charlemagne, Lebègue Bichot et Cie 1964

Les 3 Dômes, Hotel Sofitel

Lyon, France

Chef: Marc Alix

HOMARD GRILLE CARDINAL
(Broiled Lobster with Cognac Sauce)

- 2 live lobsters
- 1 tablespoon olive oil
- ¼ cup finely chopped shallots
- 1 tablespoon mashed truffle
- 3 tablespoons cognac
- ¼ cup heavy cream
  Salt and freshly ground pepper to taste

Split the lobsters lengthwise. Remove the sac behind the head and reserve the coral and tomalley. Season each lobster half with salt and pepper.

Over a high flame, heat the lobsters in a pan with olive oil until flesh is firm and shells are red. Then put them on a plate and keep warm. In the meantime, strain the coral and tomalley through a fine sieve. Add the shallots, mashed truffle, cognac and cream. Season with salt and pepper.

Place this mixture in a saucepan over a very low flame and stir it with a wooden spoon until sauce is smooth and nicely red-colored (cardinal). Do not bring to a boil—it should be only half-cooked.

Place the lobster halves under a hot broiler for about 15 minutes. Baste them three times with the sauce.

Serves: 4

Wine: Corton-Charlemagne 1967

Gaston et Gastounette

Cannes, France

Chef: Daniel Rouvière

LANGOUSTE A L'IMPERIALE
(Lobster in Curried Orange Sauce)

- 4 1-pound (500-gram) live lobsters
  Salt and freshly ground pepper to taste
- 1 cup julienne carrots
- 1 cup chopped onion
- 1 cup peeled, seeded tomatoes
- 2 tablespoons cognac
- 1½ cups fish stock
- 1 cup dry white wine
- 2 tablespoons tomato sauce
- 6 tablespoons mild curry powder, or to taste
- 1 cup heavy cream
- ¾ cup Benedictine
  Juice of 3 oranges
- ½ cup blanched, slivered orange peel
- ½ cup sliced truffles

Cut up live lobsters. Remove tomalley and coral and put them aside. Season the pieces with salt and pepper. Place in a pan containing the vegetables. Flame with cognac. Add fish stock, white wine and tomato sauce and let boil for 20 minutes. Remove lobster pieces and keep warm. Mix coral and tomalley with curry, cream, Benedictine and orange juice and pour over the lobster pieces; boil down the liquid for 20 minutes. Stir lightly, strain sauce and place in sauceboat with orange peel and truffle slices. Serve with rice, if desired.

Serves: 4

Wine: Graves

Mirabelle
London, England
Chef: John Drees

HOMARD MIRABELLE

(Lobster Mirabelle)

    2 1½-pound (750-gram) live lobsters
    ¾ cup finely chopped carrots
    ¾ cup finely chopped celery
    ¼ cup finely chopped shallots
    ¾ cup butter
    ¼ cup dry white wine
    ¼ cup cognac
      Salt and freshly ground pepper to taste
    ½ cup heavy cream
    1 egg yolk
    ¼ cup bread crumbs

Split lobsters lengthwise. Place carrots, celery and shallots in casserole with half the butter. Lay lobsters on top and add wine, cognac, salt and pepper. Cover pan, bring to a boil, then bake in a hot (400° F.) oven for 20 minutes.

Remove lobsters, break claws and take off shell. Place claws on top of lobster and keep warm. Add cream to stock and reduce until it has thickened. This should take about 7 minutes on brisk heat. Remove from heat and add the rest of the butter and the egg yolk, whisking well. Pour sauce over lobsters and sprinkle bread crumbs on top. Put under grill until crumbs color.

Serves: 6

Wine: Chassagne-Montrachet Château de la Maltroys 1967

Four Seasons and Vintage Room
London, England
Chef: R. Bellone

CHICKEN AND LOBSTER

    2 2-pound (1-kilogram) live lobsters
    4 large chicken legs
    ½ cup butter
    ½ cup brandy
    4 cups Lobster Sauce (see index)
    ½ cup heavy cream

Remove shells from lobsters and skin from chicken legs. Cut lobsters and chicken into 1-inch cubes and cook together in water to cover for 10 minutes. Then, at the table, sauté chicken and lobster pieces in butter in a chafing dish for about 2 minutes. Flame with brandy. Mix Lobster Sauce and cream together and pour over lobster and chicken. Stir together over a hot flame. Serve immediately with rice pilaf, if desired.

Serves: 4

Wine: Chassagne-Montrachet le Cru Delagrange 1967/1968

Sabatini

Florence, Italy

Chef: Francesco Focardi

ARAGOSTA IN BELLAVISTA

(Cold Lobster Mayonnaise)

1 4-pound (2-kilogram) live lobster
¼ cup sweet butter, softened
2 tablespoons unflavored gelatin
1½ cups fish stock or light chicken broth
1 cup mayonnaise
   Black truffle slices or ripe olives

Boil the lobster; let it cool. Place the lobster on its back. Carefully remove intestinal sac. Leave green liver. Remove a little of the roe and set aside for decoration. Slit the membrane on the bottom of the tail and remove meat in one piece. From the thickest part, cut four slices (medallions). Spread the tail shell with butter and replace the remaining meat in it. Put medallions and lobster in refrigerator to chill thoroughly.

Soften the gelatin in ¼ cup cold water. Bring 2 tablespoons stock or consommé to a boil and add half the softened gelatin. When gelatin is completely dissolved, let it cool and mix into mayonnaise. Chill until almost set. Melt the other half of the gelatin in the remaining stock. Chill until it begins to thicken.

Place the chilled medallions on a wire rack over a bowl. Spoon the mayonnaise over them. Chill. Repeat. Just before mayonnaise is set, dip truffle slices or olives into thickened stock and decorate medallions with them. When thoroughly chilled, top truffle slices with bits of roe. Chill again. Spoon thickened stock over decorated medallions and let set.

When medallions are thoroughly jellied, arrange lobster attractively on a wire rack over a bowl. Spoon thickened stock over it. Chill. Repeat. Garnish with decorated medallions dipped in jellied stock. Finally, spoon thickened stock over all. Chill until thoroughly set.

To serve, carefully transfer lobster to platter. Decorate dish with greens, fresh vegetables and eggs in aspic, if desired.

Serves: 4

Wine: Pinot de Francia Corta or Monte Carlo

Oesterbar
Amsterdam, Netherlands
Chef: M. Moet

La Chèvre d'Or
Eze Village, France
Chef: Vincent Barone

COLD LOBSTER IN THE BAG

¼ cup chopped leeks
¼ cup chopped onion
¼ cup chopped carrot
¼ cup chopped celery
1 bay leaf
1 tablespoon crushed peppercorns
1 sprig thyme
4 threads saffron
1 teaspoon salt
1 1-pound (500-gram) live lobster
3 cups dry white wine
½ head lettuce, shredded
1 lemon, thinly sliced
1 slice smoked salmon
2 slices toast, cut in triangles
1 tablespoon caviar
1 hard-cooked egg, sliced
¼ cup capers
1 tablespoon buttered bread crumbs

Tie leek, onion, carrot, celery, bay leaf, peppercorns, thyme, saffron and salt together in a piece of muslin. Boil lobster in wine and water to cover, together with the bag of vegetables, for about 12 minutes. Leave it in cooking liquid to cool. Put cold lobster on a serving dish on a bed of lettuce. Garnish with lemon slices, salmon on toast, caviar, egg slices and capers. Sprinkle with bread crumbs.

Serves: 2

Wine: Chablis Grand Cru Mouton 1960

LOBSTER "CHEVRE D'OR"

2 1-pound (500-gram) live rock lobsters
  Salt and freshly ground pepper to taste
½ cup butter
¼ cup sauce Américaine (rich tomato sauce)
¼ cup velouté au champagne (white sauce made with light stock and champagne)
¾ cup heavy cream

Split the lobsters. Salt and pepper them, dot with butter and bake until almost done, about 12 minutes, in a hot (400° F.) oven. Meanwhile mix sauce Américaine, velouté au champagne and cream; pour over lobsters. Return to oven and bake 5 minutes more. (Shells will turn red when done.)

Serves: 2

Wine: Champagne

FEM SMÅ HUS
Stockholm, Sweden
Scampi Indiana
(page 166)

MIRABELLE
London, England
Chef: John Drees
Homard Mirabelle
(page 158)

KALASTAJATORPPA
Helsinki, Finland
Chef: Kalervo Paakkinen
Burbot Pasty Cabane
(page 148)

Carlton
Brussels, Belgium
Chef: Julien Vermersch

HOMARD AUX AROMATES
(Aromatic Lobster)

3 cups dry white wine
1 tablespoon salt
10 peppercorns
  Pinch thyme
1 bay leaf
2 cloves garlic
1 cup chopped onions
1 carrot, diced
1 shallot, chopped
6 sprigs parsley
1 cup chopped celery
2 live lobsters
1 carrot, sliced
½ cup French-cut green beans
1½ tablespoons flour
1½ tablespoons soft butter
½ cup heavy cream
¼ cup minced parsley

In a large kettle, bring to a boil 2 cups water, wine, salt, peppercorns, thyme, bay leaf, garlic, half the onion, diced carrot, shallot, parsley and celery. Reduce heat and simmer 15 minutes. Bring to a boil again and add lobsters; cook about 15 minutes—shells will turn bright red when lobsters are done. Remove lobsters and set aside.

Reduce stock by half. Strain; discard cooked-out vegetables. Cook sliced carrot, the rest of the onion and the green beans in stock until just tender-crisp.

Strain and keep vegetables warm. Blend flour and butter together; add to stock and cook 5 minutes. Reduce to simmering; add cream and continue cooking gently until sauce is thickened. Adjust seasonings.

Cut lobsters in two lengthwise. Remove intestinal sac but leave green liver and any roe. Arrange on a heatproof serving platter and cover with sauce. Run under broiler until sauce is bubbling. Garnish with cooked vegetables and parsley and serve at once.

Serves: 2

Wine: Pouilly-Fuissé

O'Pescador
Cascais, Portugal
Chef: Paulo Marcelino Dias

LAGOSTA GRELHADA
(Broiled Lobster)

2 2-pound (1-kilogram) live lobsters
½ cup butter, melted
  Salt to taste
  Juice of ½ lemon
4 baked potatoes

Split lobsters lengthwise; clean, brush with melted butter and broil for 20 minutes. Season remaining butter with salt and lemon juice and pour over lobster. Serve with baked potatoes.

Serves: 4

Normandie Restaurant
Birtle (near Bury), England
Chef: J. P. Champeau

HOMARD "CHAMPEAU"

(Lobster with Pernod)

2 2¼-pound (1-kilogram) live lobsters
  Salt and freshly ground pepper to taste
1 tablespoon olive oil
2 tablespoons butter
¾ cup Pernod
4 cloves garlic, chopped
½ cup chopped shallots
1 cup cognac
1 tablespoon chopped parsley

Cut lobsters in half and season with salt and pepper. Heat oil and butter in pan until sizzling; add lobsters, cover pan and simmer slowly for 10 minutes. Turn lobsters; add Pernod, garlic and shallots and continue cooking, uncovered, for another 3 minutes. Pour cognac over lobsters and flame. Arrange lobsters on a silver dish. Add parsley to the sauce and pour over lobsters. This dish must be prepared at the last minute and served at once.

Serves: 4

Wine: Champagne or Côtes du Rhone blanc

Wheeler's
London, England
Chef: S. F. Chu

LOBSTER NEWBURG

2 1½-pound (750-gram) live lobsters
6 tablespoons butter
6 tablespoons brandy
¾ cup Madeira
1¼ cups heavy cream
2 egg yolks, beaten
2 cups cooked rice

Place lobsters in 1 quart boiling water and boil for 20 minutes. Remove lobsters from their cooking liquid and split from head to tail. Remove the sac behind the head and the intestine (a thin gray or black line) in the tail. Remove meat from shells and slice into 1-inch-long pieces. Heat butter and lightly sauté the lobster. Flame with brandy. Remove lobster pieces and reserve. Add Madeira to pan and simmer for about 10 minutes, or until it is reduced to about ½ cup. Add all but 2 tablespoons cream. Simmer, stirring constantly, until sauce begins to thicken. Remove from heat and beat in egg yolks. Add the remaining cream, return to heat and simmer until sauce is thick. Do not allow to boil. Place hot cooked rice on a serving dish and arrange lobster meat, topped with sauce, on it. Serve immediately.

Serves: 4

Wine: Chablis Premier Cru Beau Royal 1969

The Mirabeau
Dun Laóghaire
County Dublin, Ireland
Chef: Patrick Rafferty

LOBSTER DELMONICO

  4 large live lobsters
  1 tablespoon butter
  2 shallots, finely chopped
1¼ cups fish velouté
  1 tablespoon tomato purée
1¼ cups heavy cream
  1 tablespoon brandy
     Juice of 1 lemon
  2 tablespoons tomato concassée
     Poached roe of lobster (if available)
  1 lemon, cut in wedges

Split lobsters, remove flesh and dice. Heat pan and add butter and shallots; sauté for a few seconds. Add fish velouté, lobster flesh, tomato purée, cream, half the brandy and the lemon juice, stirring gently until thoroughly blended. Arrange shells on salver. After filling the shells with the prepared mixture, decorate with tomato concassée and roe. Brown lightly under broiler. Flame with the rest of the brandy and serve with wedges of lemon.

Serves: 6

Wine: Chablis or Pouilly-Fuissé

Estalagem Muchaxo
Cascais, Portugal
Chef: Joao de Brito

LAGOSTA A MUCHAXO
(Lobster, Muchaxo's Way)

  3 1½-pound (750-gram) live lobsters
  2 medium onions, peeled and chopped
  2 tablespoons olive oil
  3 cups tomato sauce
 ½ cup butter
  1 cup cognac

Cut up lobsters in thick pieces. Fry the onions in olive oil until well browned. Add tomato sauce and simmer for 10 minutes. Fry the lobster pieces in their shells in butter for about 5 minutes. Place on flameproof platter or tray; warm the cognac, pour over and flame. Place lobster pieces in tomato sauce and simmer gently for 15 minutes. Serve over fluffy rice, if desired.

Serves: 4

Chez Puget (Le Petit Brouant)
Nice, France
Chef: Gaston Puget

COCKTAIL DE GROSSES CREVETTES DITES GAMBEROTES

(Shrimp Cocktail)

- 6 large or 12 small shrimp
- 1 teaspoon salt
- 10 crushed peppercorns
- ¼ cup mayonnaise
- 1 tablespoon catsup
- 1 tablespoon cognac
  Salt and freshly ground pepper to taste
- 2 lemon quarters
- ½ cup shredded lettuce

Poach shrimp in salted water with peppercorns for 5 minutes. Cool enough to handle; shell (leave tips of tails on two shrimp for decoration).

Mix mayonnaise with catsup and cognac; season with salt and pepper.

Place lettuce on bottom of cocktail cup. Arrange all but two shrimp with tails on lettuce and cover with mayonnaise sauce. Decorate with two remaining shrimp and two small quarters of lemon.

Serves: 1

Wine: Blanc che Bellit

Hotel Ambassador
Opatija, Yugoslavia
Chef: Ilija Šustić

GRILLED SHRIMP OF THE ADRIATIC

- 8 servings raw shrimp in shells
- 2 lemons, thinly sliced

Grill shrimp over charcoal (or under the broiler). Turn often to make sure the shells do not scorch before the shrimp are done.

To serve, decorate each portion of shrimp with lemon slices. Fried rice or a pilaf is usually served with grilled shrimp on the Adriatic coast. Tartar sauce is optional.

Serves: 8

On the Rocks
Varkiza, Athens, Greece
Chef: Nicolas Loudaras

SHRIMP ON A SPIT

    1 cup thick mayonnaise
    1 teaspoon tomato catsup
    1 teaspoon Worcestershire sauce
    1 teaspoon hot pepper sauce
    1 teaspoon whiskey
   24 extra-large shrimp, cleaned
   12 slices fat bacon or salt pork
    1 cup green pepper squares
    2 lemons, sliced
    2 sprigs parsley

Mix first five ingredients and set aside.

Roll half the shrimp in a strip of bacon each. On a spit (or skewer), place a rolled shrimp, a square of green pepper and a plain shrimp. Continue until spit is full, or all shrimp have been used. Grill for about 10 minutes, turning once by hand if spit is not automatic. Garnish with slices of lemon and parsley sprigs. Serve immediately. Pass the reserved cocktail sauce separately.

Serves: 4

Wine: Greek "Kava Kamba"

Lapérouse
Paris, France
Chef: Fernand Poisson

GRATIN DE LANGOUSTINES GEORGETTE

(Prawns "Georgette")

    2 pounds (1 kilogram) prawns or jumbo
      shrimp
    3 cups strong court bouillon
    1 cup quartered mushrooms
  5½ tablespoons chopped shallots
    1 cup butter
    2 tablespoons brandy
   ½ cup rich tomato sauce
    1 head Boston lettuce, braised
   ¾ cup white sauce flavored with white wine
  3½ tablespoons grated Parmesan cheese

Poach fresh prawns in court bouillon for 8 minutes. Drain and shell.

Simmer mushrooms and shallots in butter over a low flame. When the mushrooms are done, add the shelled prawns. Deglaze the pan with brandy and blend in tomato sauce.

Arrange mushrooms, prawns and braised lettuce on an au gratin dish; pour the white wine sauce over it. Sprinkle with grated Parmesan cheese and glaze under the broiler. Serve very hot.

Serves: 4

Wine: Chassagne Marquis de la Guiche 1959

Fem Små Hus

Stockholm, Sweden

SCAMPI INDIANA

1¼ cups raw langoustine tails, shelled
¼ cup butter
1 tablespoon curry powder
1 clove garlic, pressed
Salt and freshly ground white pepper to taste
2 dashes hot pepper sauce
¼ cup cognac
2 tomatoes, cut into quarters
½ cup chopped pimientos
½ lettuce heart, finely shredded

Sauté langoustine tails briskly in half the butter for about 5 minutes. Add curry, garlic, salt, pepper and hot pepper sauce. Heat while stirring. Pour cognac over this and flame. Add tomato quarters, pimientos and finely shredded lettuce. Simmer for about 10 minutes, or until thickened. If desired, additional seasoning may be added. Stir in remaining butter just before serving. Serve with rice, if desired.

Serves: 2

Pfeffermühle

Basel, Switzerland

Chef: Jean Carlo Erba

SCAMPI A LA JEAN CARLO

5 to 7 medium scampi
Juice of ½ lemon
Salt and freshly ground pepper to taste
1 teaspoon very finely chopped pimiento
¼ teaspoon tarragon or marjoram
¾ cup melted butter or oil
1 tablespoon dry mustard
1 cup heavy cream
Salt and freshly ground pepper to taste
1 tablespoon lemon juice

Cut scampi in half lengthwise with scissors or knife; break off tails and remove intestines. Draw scampi onto a skewer, tail first; mix lemon juice, salt, pepper, pimiento and tarragon or marjoram and spread on scampi. Let stand for about 15 minutes; then brush with melted butter or oil and grill over moderate heat (or broil under moderate flame).

Mix mustard and cream. Season with salt, pepper and lemon juice. Serve cold sauce over hot scampi. Pass extra sauce.

Serves: 1

Wine: Aigle les Murailles or Chante Alouette (Hermitage)

Terrazza
London, England
Chef: Carlo Avogadri

FUSILLI MARIO FRANCO

(Fusilli with Seafood Sauce)

¼ **cup butter**
¼ **pound (120 grams) shelled scampi (jumbo shrimp), cut small**
¼ **pound (120 grams) calamari (squid), cleaned and cut small**
2 **sea scallops, cut small**
Salt and freshly ground pepper to taste
2 **tablespoons brandy**
2 **threads saffron**
¾ **cup heavy cream**
Salt and freshly ground pepper to taste
½ **pound (250 grams) fusilli (short, twisted, thick pasta)**
2 **tablespoons butter**

Melt butter in saucepan over medium heat; then add chopped seafood and season to taste. Cook fish slowly until all liquid has evaporated. Add brandy to fish and flame. Add saffron and mix well; then add cream. Check seasoning; reduce until sauce is thick (about three-quarters of original volume). Remove from heat.

Bring 2 quarts of salted water to a boil. Add fusilli and cook for 8 to 10 minutes, or just until pasta is barely tender. Do not cover pan. When done, drain fusilli well, return to saucepan, add butter and toss to coat. Top with sauce. Mix well and serve.

Serves: 2

Wine: Bolla Bardolino

George's
Rome, Italy
Chef: Bruno Croce

SCAMPI FLAMBES AU WHISKY

(Scampi Flamed with Scotch Whisky)

4 **pounds (2 kilograms) scampi in shells**
1 **cup rice**
½ **cup clarified butter***
Salt and freshly ground pepper to taste
¼ **cup Scotch whisky**

Cook scampi in about 4 quarts of boiling water, highly salted, for 8 minutes. Shell them and keep warm. Boil rice for about 20 minutes and keep hot.

Melt clarified butter in a chafing dish; when hot, add scampi, salt and pepper. Keep the pan on the heat for 30 seconds—just long enough to warm the scampi thoroughly (they must not fry). Add whisky, warm again and flame, shaking pan to burn whisky completely. Serve on bed of hot rice together with the pan juices.

Serves: 4

*Clarifying the butter is extremely important because it gives the scampi a very delicate flavor completely different from the one given by fresh butter.

Wine: Villa Antinori bianco

Restaurant de la Mère Guy
Lyon, France
Chef: Roger Roucou

CRAYFISH TAILS AU GRATIN

4½ pounds (2.25 kilograms) crayfish
2 cups butter
2 cups heavy cream
2 tablespoons Hollandaise Sauce (see index)

Drop crayfish into boiling water and boil 10 minutes; then drop them into cold water. Remove the tails from the shell. Crush shells and braise them in a hot (400° F.) oven with butter. Remove from oven and pour shell-butter over hot water so that the butter, red and full of the flavor of the crayfish, comes to the surface. Take it out with a ladle and clarify. Add the crayfish tails and heat just enough to make them firm. Reserve. Pour cream into butter and reduce by one-third. Remove from flame; add Hollandaise Sauce. Place crayfish into an au gratin dish, nap with sauce and glaze under the broiler at serving time.

Serves: 4

Wine: Meursault Goutte d'Or

Hostellerie du Cerf
Marlenheim, France
Chef: Robert Husser

CRAYFISH MOLD "BRILLAT-SAVARIN"

2 dozen crayfish
½ cup butter
2 tablespoons dry champagne
½ cup chopped shallots
½ cup diced carrots
½ cup minced parsley stems
1½ cups Riesling
½ cup veal stock
2 tomatoes, peeled, seeded and chopped
Salt to taste
Thyme
Cayenne
¼ cup heavy cream

Remove the intestinal tracts from crayfish (red legs). Brown the crayfish lightly in hot butter. Deglaze pan with champagne and flame. Add shallots, carrots and parsley stems to pan. Add Riesling, veal stock, tomatoes, salt, thyme and cayenne to taste. Cover and simmer for 10 minutes to reduce liquid by half. Remove crayfish and put them into a mold. Add heavy cream to the sauce, reduce again, correct the seasonings and pour sauce over the crayfish.

Serves: 4

Wine: Gewurtztraminer

Lucas Carton
Paris, France
Chef: Comey

CASSOLETTE DE QUEUES D'ECREVISSES

(Crayfish Ragout)

6½ pounds (3.25 kilograms) crayfish
1 cup Mirepoix (recipe follows)
   Butter
   Salt and freshly ground pepper to taste
   Pinch cayenne
½ cup cognac
2 cups dry white wine
1 cup fish stock
3 medium tomatoes, peeled, seeded and chopped
2 tablespoons tomato purée
3 tablespoons flour
3 tablespoons butter
¼ cup heavy cream
¼ cup butter
½ cup truffle slices

Brown crayfish with Mirepoix in butter; season with salt, pepper and cayenne. Ignite with cognac and moisten with wine and fish stock. Add tomatoes and tomato purée. Cook for 10 minutes. Remove crayfish and shell them; keep the tails warm in a covered pot. To make sauce, crush shells through a fine mesh sieve, add to liquid and boil down by half. Knead flour and butter and blend with shells. Add cream and beat in ¼ cup butter. Check seasonings. Place the crayfish tails in an au gratin casserole; pour the sauce over it and glaze quickly under the broiler. Decorate with truffle slices.

Mirepoix

¼ cup chopped carrots
¼ cup chopped onion
¼ cup chopped celery
1 tablespoon chopped fennel
1 tablespoon chopped thyme
1 bay leaf

Combine all ingredients thoroughly.

Serves: 4

Cladagh Grillroom
Galway, Ireland
Chef: Patrick Duignan

GALWAY BAY SCALLOPS A LA MAISON

8 large scallops in shells
1¼ cups dry white wine
½ cup sliced mushrooms
6 tablespoons finely chopped onion
1 tablespoon chopped parsley
⅓ cup heavy cream
3 tablespoons flour
3 tablespoons butter
   Salt and freshly ground pepper to taste
3 cups potato purée

Shell scallops, reserving the shells, and clean. Then place in 1¼ cups water with wine, mushrooms, onion and parsley. Cook for 12 to 15 minutes. Remove scallops and add cream to stock. Reduce by about one-third. Blend flour and butter and add to thicken; cook 5 minutes. Season with salt and pepper. Clean and dry shells; pipe potato around edges. Place scallops in shells and cover with sauce.

Serves: 4

Wine: **Puligny-Montrachet, les Combettes**

Wheeler's

London, England

Chef: S. F. Chu

OYSTERS MORNAY

As many as 4 dozen oysters, depending on whether allowing 6, 9 or 12 per person
2½ **cups béchamel sauce**
1 **cup grated Parmesan cheese**
½ **cup heavy cream**

Shell oysters and simmer them in their own juice for a few minutes. Dry inside of lower shells and return cooked oysters to them. Add warm oyster-cooking juice to the béchamel and stir in ½ cup of cheese. Heat slowly; when thoroughly mixed, add cream. Pour sauce over oysters and sprinkle remaining cheese on top. Place under the broiler for a few minutes until top is brown. Serve immediately.

Serves: 4

Wine: Chablis Premier Cru Beau Royal 1969

Overton's

London, England

Chef: Carl Lerner

MUSSEL-AND-OYSTER STEW OVERTON

6 **dozen large mussels in shells**
6 **chopped shallots**
1¼ **cups dry white wine**
¼ **cup butter**
¼ **cup flour**
3 **dozen oysters, shelled**
2 **egg yolks**
¼ **cup heavy cream**
6 **cups Duchesse Potatoes (see index)**
1 **cup cooked, diced carrots**
1 **cup cooked green peas**

Wash and brush mussels well and place in a casserole with chopped shallots. Add white wine and bring to a boil. When shells have opened, remove from heat and remove mussels from shells.

Mix butter and flour together and add remaining mussel stock. Place on low heat and add mussels and oysters. Stir in egg yolks and cream and serve in a ring of creamy but firm Duchesse Potatoes. Garnish with diced carrots and peas.

Serves: 6

Wine: Extra dry champagne

Tiberio
London, England
Chef: Leoni Cristiani

COZZE GRATINATE
(Baked Mussels with Garlic)

  36 large mussels, scraped, washed and dried
     Salt and freshly ground pepper to taste
   1 teaspoon lemon juice
   6 tablespoons fresh white bread crumbs
   2 cloves garlic, finely chopped
   1 sprig parsley, chopped
   5 tablespoons olive oil
   4 lemon wedges

Open mussels (as oysters), leaving in the half shell. Place in a baking dish; add salt, pepper and lemon juice. Mix bread crumbs, garlic and parsley together and sprinkle mixture liberally over mussels until thoroughly covered. Sprinkle oil over all and bake in a hot (425° F.) oven for 7 to 10 minutes, according to size of mussels. Remove and place on serving dish. Decorate with lemon wedges.

Serves: 2

Wine: Verdicchio Fazi Battaglia

Wheeler's Sovereign
London, England
Chef: Man Ying Sau

MOULES A LA MARINIERE
(Mussels, Mariner's-Style)

  10 cups mussels in shells
  ¼ cup finely chopped shallots
  ¼ cup chopped parsley
     Pinch freshly ground pepper
  ½ cup dry white wine
  ¼ cup butter
  ½ cup heavy cream
  ¼ cup chopped parsley

Wash mussels thoroughly in several changes of water. Scrub thoroughly to remove all grit. Place mussels in large, covered saucepan. Add shallots, ¼ cup parsley and pepper. Pour in wine and 2 cups water; simmer, covered, over high heat. As soon as shells have opened, remove pan from heat. Place mussels in a serving dish and remove top shells. To the cooking liquid, add butter, cream and parsley. Boil rapidly together for 2 or 3 minutes and pour over mussels. Sprinkle with additional parsley, if desired, and serve immediately.

Serves: 4

Wine: Puligny-Montrachet les Folatières 1967

Section Eight

RICE, SALADS, VEGETABLES AND PASTA

Ristorante Savini

Milan, Italy

Chef: Sante Guerini

RISOTTO ALLA MILANESE

¼ **cup finely chopped onion**

¼ **cup butter**

1 **cup short-grained rice**

2 **teaspoons dried saffron**

¼ **cup dry white wine**

1 **cup chicken broth**

2 **tablespoons butter**

¼ **cup grated Parmesan cheese**

In a medium saucepan, sauté onion in butter until lightly browned. Add rice and stir until rice turns milky-white, about 5 minutes. Soften saffron in a little water and add to rice and onion mixture, stirring well. Spoon wine over the rice and let it simmer until liquid has evaporated. Add the hot chicken broth a little at a time—the rice should be barely covered by chicken broth all the time it is being added. This takes about 15 to 18 minutes. The rice must not be allowed to cook vigorously. Remove the pan from the heat and, before serving, add 2 tablespoons butter and Parmesan cheese.

Serves: 2

Wine: Bardolino-Chiaretto

Ristorante Savini

Milan, Italy

Chef: Sante Guerini

RISOTTO AL SALTO

1 **teaspoon butter**

Risotto alla Milanese (see this page)

For Risotto al Salto, use only Risotto alla Milanese (without Parmesan) which has been cooked not less than 6 hours before. Put Risotto alla Milanese into an iron frying pan with about 1 teaspoon butter (just enough to prevent rice from sticking). Cook over medium heat. With a spatula or spoon, push the rice into a mound. Wait about 3 minutes. Prevent rice mound from sticking by shaking the pan and tossing rice. Wait a further 3 minutes and Risotto al Salto is ready. Let the risotto slide onto a very hot dish and serve.

Serves: 1

Wine: Bardolino-Chiaretto

Tiberio

London, England

Chef: Leoni Cristiani

INSALATA CESARE
(Caesar Salad)

    1 head romaine (cos lettuce)
    1 avocado
    1 orange, peeled
    1 slice pineapple
    1 piece heart of palm (palmito)
    1 bunch watercress
    1 tablespoon toasted almond halves
      Vinaigrette Dressing (recipe follows)

Use only heart of romaine; wash, dry and cut it into fairly small pieces. Peel and cut avocado into slices. Quarter the orange. Cut the pineapple slice into scallops and the piece of palmito into rounds. Wash and dry watercress; cut off and discard any tough stems. Arrange all ingredients in salad bowl and sprinkle with almonds. Serve with Vinaigrette Dressing.

Vinaigrette Dressing

    3 tablespoons olive oil
    ½ tablespoon white wine vinegar
    1 tablespoon orange juice
      Pinch oregano
      Salt and freshly ground pepper to taste

Shake ingredients together and chill well before using.

Serves: 2

Trader Vic's

London, England

Chef: Oswald Mair

CHICKEN SALAD HAWAIIAN

    ½ cup diced dark meat of chicken
    ½ cup diced white meat of chicken
    ½ cup diced celery
    2 tablespoons mayonnaise
      Salt and freshly ground white pepper to taste
    1 teaspoon mai kai (monosodium glutamate)
    2 slices pineapple
      Papaya chunks
      Melon balls
      Sliced strawberries
    ¼ cup honey
    1 teaspoon lemon juice

Mix chicken, celery, mayonnaise, salt, pepper and mai kai lightly. Arrange on an oval platter and garnish with halves of pineapple circles, papaya chunks and melon balls. Top with sliced strawberries. Thin honey with lemon juice. Serve in a small sauceboat. This sauce should be poured over entire salad.

Serves: 1

Taverna Ta Nissia, Athens Hilton Hotel
Athens, Greece
Chef: Manfred Bertele

AVOCADO "CAP SOUNION"

1½ tablespoons butter
1½ tablespoons chopped onion
1¼ cups raw shrimp, shelled
  2 tablespoons dry white wine
  1 sprig saffron
     Salt and freshly ground pepper to taste
3½ tablespoons mushroom pieces
  7 tablespoons mayonnaise
  1 tablespoon catsup
     Salt and freshly ground pepper to taste
½   teaspoon Worcestershire sauce
  2 avocados, halved
  4 ripe olives
  1 hard-cooked egg, sliced
  1 tomato, quartered
  4 sprigs parsley

Melt butter in saucepan, add onion and sauté very slowly for 10 minutes. Add shrimp and sauté for 10 minutes more. Add white wine and ½ cup water; simmer 5 minutes. Season with saffron, salt and pepper, and boil for 8 minutes. Remove shrimp and set aside to cool. Reduce liquid to about 1 tablespoon.

Cut shrimp in pieces. Combine with mushrooms, mayonnaise, 1 tablespoon of the reduced liquid and catsup. Season to taste with salt, pepper and Worcestershire sauce.

Fill avocado halves with mixture. Garnish with olives, egg slices, tomato wedges and parsley sprigs.

Serves: 4

Wine: Santa Helena

Les Mésanges
Montbonnot (Isère), France
Chef: G. Achini

GRATIN DE CARDONS
(Cardoons in White Sauce)

4½ pounds (2.25 kilograms) cardoons*
     Juice of 1 lemon
  2 teaspoons salt
  1 tablespoon flour
½   cup veal fat
  1 cup white sauce
     Veal or poultry stock
     Salt and freshly ground pepper to taste
     Nutmeg
     Butter
½   cup grated Gruyère or Beaufort cheese
½   cup butter or fat of goose liver

The cardoons should be very white. Pare off the outer fibers; cut the stalks into 3- to 4-inch pieces, dropping them into 3 cups water with the lemon juice to prevent darkening. Boil the cardoons in 3 cups water to which salt, flour and veal fat have been added (this is to keep the cardoons very white).

In the meantime, thin white sauce with veal or poultry stock. Season well with salt, pepper and a little nutmeg. Drain the cardoons, place them in a buttered au gratin pan and pour the sauce over them. Sprinkle with grated Gruyère or Beaufort cheese and dot with pieces of butter—or better still with fat of goose liver. Place in a hot (400° F.) oven. Serve piping hot.

Serves: 4

*A vegetable belonging to the artichoke family, shaped like a giant bunch of celery—ribs and leaves edible.

Wine: Côte-Rôtie

Chateau de Madrid
Villefranche sur Mer, France
Chef: Sarti

TARTE AUX ARTICHAUTS
(Artichoke Tart)

```
20   artichokes
     Juice of 2 lemons
¼    cup oil
¼    cup butter
     Salt and freshly ground pepper to taste
1⅛   cups pâte feuilletée (flaky pastry)
¼    cup Mornay Sauce (recipe follows)
 6   eggs
     Salt and freshly ground pepper to taste
```

Clean the artichokes, keeping only the hearts. Drop them as they are cleaned into water and lemon juice to avoid blackening. (Thawed frozen artichoke hearts can be used instead.) When ready to cook, drain hearts, cut them into fine slices and sauté them in oil and butter until tender and light brown. Add salt and pepper.

Roll out flaky pastry very thin. Place on a cookie sheet and form a border about ½-inch high all around pastry by folding edge under and fluting with fingers. Prick pastry shell with a fork and bake in a moderate (350° F.) oven for 20 minutes.

Spread the shell with Mornay Sauce; top with artichokes. Make six wells in filling and break an egg into each. Season and place in oven until eggs are set.

Mornay Sauce

```
 2   tablespoons butter
 2   tablespoons flour
¾    cup milk
     Salt and white pepper to taste
½    cup grated Gruyère cheese
```

Melt butter in top of double boiler. Add flour and cook for 5 minutes. Add milk and stir while sauce thickens. Season with salt and pepper. Add cheese and stir to blend in thoroughly.

Serves: 6

Wine: Chablis

Grand Hotel

Brno, Czechoslovakia

STUFFED MUSHROOMS

```
 1   pound (500 grams) venison, cooked and
     ground
¼    cup minced onion
 1   egg
     Salt and freshly ground pepper to taste
 1   teaspoon cognac
 2   tablespoons butter, melted
20   large mushroom caps
 5   strips bacon, halved
 2   tablespoons flour
 3   eggs, lightly beaten
 2   tablespoons bread crumbs
 1   tablespoon oil
```

Mix venison, onion and 1 egg. Add salt, pepper, cognac and butter. Stuff mushroom caps with mixture, press two caps together, wrap in a bacon slice. Roll in flour, dip in beaten eggs, then roll in bread crumbs. Sauté in heated oil for about 5 minutes, rolling them around to cook bacon.

Serves: 10

Don Salvatore
Naples, Italy
Chef: Giovanni Uliano

SPAGHETTI "COSA NOSTRA"

¼ cup salt
¾ pound spaghetti
1 clove garlic
6 tablespoons olive oil
2 large crayfish in shells
1 tomato, peeled, seeded and chopped
1 dozen clams in shells
1 dozen mussels in shells
2 sprigs parsley

To make the spaghetti, boil 4 quarts of water to which the salt has been added. When water has come to a boil, add spaghetti and simmer for 7 minutes. Test for doneness (different spaghettis require different cooking times). Drain as soon as pasta is done. Do not rinse. Serve at once —sauce should be ready when spaghetti is done.

To make the sauce, fry garlic in olive oil. Add the crayfish and tomato. Cook 5 minutes; then add the clams and mussels. When the clams and mussels open (about 5 minutes), add sprigs of parsley. The sauce is ready when it has a "bright" appearance.

Serves: 2

Wine: Capri white

El Sombrero
Naples, Italy
Chef: Mario Corvo

SPAGHETTI "MARIUS"

½ cup diced thick lean bacon
¼ cup butter
1 teaspoon vinegar
2 cups boiled spaghetti
¼ cup grated Parmesan cheese
¼ cup beef gravy
¼ cup cream or milk
4 egg yolks, lightly beaten
Freshly ground pepper to taste

Braise bacon in butter until crisp; add vinegar. When it evaporates, add spaghetti and mix well. Add cheese and continue mixing over moderate heat. Add gravy, then cream and then eggs, mixing after each addition. Continue mixing and cooking for 2 or 3 minutes. Serve immediately on hot plates. Grind pepper over each serving.

Serves: 4

Wine: Capri white

Section Nine

*EGGS, CREPES, PANCAKES
AND SOUFFLES*

Hotel Pension Schwarzenberg

Vienna, Austria

POACHED EGGS "SCHWARZENBERG"

6 slices goose liver pâté
6 pieces round toast
6 poached eggs
1 cup Hollandaise Sauce (see index)
2 tablespoons catsup
6 truffles, sliced

Place a slice of goose liver pâté on each piece of toast. Place poached eggs over the pâté. Color Hollandaise Sauce a light pink with catsup. Cover the entire preparation with Hollandaise Sauce. Garnish top with strips of truffles. Before serving, warm in the oven for about 1 minute.

Serves: 3

Hôtel Plaza Athénée

Paris, France

Chef: Jean Plet

CREPES FARCIES BOCCADOR

(Stuffed Pancakes)

8 large fresh or canned crab legs
¼ cup butter
   Salt and freshly ground pepper to taste
½ cup cognac or fine champagne
½ cup rich dark tomato sauce
¼ cup heavy cream
8 thin pancakes (see "Crêpes" in index)
1 tablespoon chopped parsley
1 tablespoon French mustard
1 cup Mornay Sauce (see index)
¼ cup grated Gruyère cheese

Cook crab legs in butter until they have given out their juice; season with salt and pepper.

Flame in cognac or fine champagne. Add tomato sauce and cream so as to thicken the whole; heat slowly.

Prepare small thin pancakes, adding chopped parsley to the batter.

Spread each pancake lightly with French mustard. Coat crab legs thickly with sauce and place one leg on each pancake. Roll up carefully. Place in a very lightly buttered dish and cover with Mornay Sauce. Sprinkle with additional grated cheese. Bake in a hot (400° F.) oven just until heated through and sauce is lightly browned.

Serves: 4

Wine: Riesling Grande Réserve or Bâtard-Montrachet

Carpati

Brasov, Romania

Chef: Ion Dosu

BRASOV CROQUETTES

Pancakes

  2 eggs
 10 tablespoons flour
 ¼ cup milk

Mix all ingredients and set aside for an hour.

Filling

 2¼ cups cooked beef, lamb or veal
  1 cup olive oil
  1 cup minced onions
 ½ teaspoon salt
 ¼ teaspoon freshly ground pepper
  1 tablespoon minced parsley

Mince the meat and put through a fine sieve. Heat oil in saucepan, add onion and sauté for about 5 minutes, or until onion is soft but not browned. Add meat, cover and braise for 45 minutes. When cool, pass mixture through a fine sieve. Season with salt, pepper and parsley.

Conclusion

 ½ cup flour
  3 egg yolks, lightly beaten
 ½ cup fine bread crumbs
  2 cups tomato sauce
 ½ cup heavy cream

Prepare pancakes in a hot, lightly oiled 6-inch skillet. Roll up meat filling in pan-cakes, tucking in the ends to prevent un-rolling. Roll filled pancakes in flour, dip in beaten egg yolk and, finally, roll in bread crumbs. Brown quickly in a hot, lightly oiled skillet. Serve accompanied by hot tomato sauce and cream.

Serves: 4

Grosvenor House

London, England

Chef: Roger Couchie

CREPES FARÇIES A LA FONDUE DU FROMAGE

(Pancakes Stuffed with Cheese Fondue)

  8 thin pancakes (see "Crêpes" in index)
  1 cup cubed Cheddar cheese
 ½ cup cubed Gruyère cheese
  4 egg yolks
 ¼ cup white sauce
  1 teaspoon Worcestershire sauce
  1 teaspoon English mustard
 ¼ cup beer
  1 tomato, cut into petals
 1¼ cups heavy cream
 ¼ cup grated Parmesan cheese

Make pancakes and keep warm. Combine and heat all ingredients except tomato, cream and Parmesan, to make pancake filling. Spoon this filling onto pancakes, fold and place in a heatproof serving dish. Decorate tops of pancakes with tomato petals and cover with cream. Sprinkle with Parmesan cheese and grill until golden brown.

Serves: 4

Wine: Kirsch or other eau de vie

Lafayette

Dublin, Ireland

Chef: Roger Noblet

CREPES AUX LANGOUSTINES

(Seafood Crêpes)

1 dozen or more (depending on size) fresh prawns or jumbo shrimp

1 2-pound (1-kilogram) live lobster

2 tablespoons salad oil

2 tablespoons tomato purée

2½ cups heavy cream
   Salt and freshly ground pepper to taste

1 bay leaf

¼ cup fish stock

2 tablespoons flour

2 tablespoons butter

2 egg yolks, beaten

6 thin crêpes (see index)

¼ cup Hollandaise Sauce (see index)

2 tablespoons grated Gruyère cheese

Simmer prawns in salted water for 2 minutes; shell. Cut lobster into small pieces and sauté gently in oil for 15 minutes. When shell is bright red, add tomato purée, cream, salt, pepper, bay leaf and fish stock. Bring to a boil and simmer for 20 minutes. Remove the lobster and reserve; discard bay leaf. Blend flour with butter and add to sauce to thicken. Cook 5 minutes. Reduce heat and stir a little of the hot liquid into the egg yolks. Then add eggs to sauce. Do not allow it to boil after eggs have been added.

Reheat the prawns in a saucepan; add two-thirds of the sauce. Use this mixture as filling for crêpes. Roll up; arrange in a baking dish. Arrange lobster pieces on top of rolled crêpes. Add Hollandaise to the remaining sauce and pour over crêpes and lobster pieces. Sprinkle dish with cheese and put in a hot (400° F.) oven until the cheese melts and begins to brown lightly. Serve very hot.

Serves: 2

Wine: Meursault 1967

Restaurant Riche

Stockholm, Sweden

Chef: Gunnar Schyl

CREPES H.K.H. PRINCE BERTIL

8 thin pancakes (see "Crêpes" in index)

1¼ cups cooked, shelled shrimp

½ cup Hollandaise Sauce (see index)

2 tablespoons chopped dillweed

½ cup grated Parmesan cheese

Make pancakes and set aside. Heat shrimp in top of double boiler; mix with Hollandaise Sauce and dillweed. Fill pancakes with shrimp mixture and roll. Place in baking dish and sprinkle with Parmesan cheese. Heat in a hot (400° F.) oven until cheese melts, about 10 minutes.

Serves: 4

Leoni's Quo Vadis

London, England

CREPES VERBANO

½ cup finely chopped onions
½ cup butter
1 cup chopped shrimp
2 cups chopped lobster meat
1 small can tuna fish
1 cup thick brown stock
1 tablespoon cognac
1½ cups crêpe batter (see index)

Sauté onion in 2 tablespoons butter until brown. Add shrimp, lobster and tuna fish and continue to sauté about 3 minutes. Add stock and simmer for 15 minutes over a low flame. Add the cognac and boil rapidly for about 1 minute. Finally, beat in the remaining butter.

While sauce is cooking, make pancakes. When sauce is finished, fill pancakes and fold once. Serve immediately.

Serves: 4

Wine: Liebfraumilch Hanns Christof

Collar of Gold Restaurant

Dublin Airport, Ireland

Chef: James Doyle

PANCAKES COLLEEN

8 very thin pancakes (see "Crêpes" in index)
½ cup sliced mushrooms
¼ cup chopped onion
¼ cup butter
1 cup cooked, shelled prawns or jumbo shrimp
1 cup cooked, shelled shrimp
2½ cups Lobster Sauce (see index)
1 cup brandy
2 tablespoons grated Parmesan cheese

Make pancakes and set aside; keep warm. Sauté mushrooms and onion in butter and add prawns and shrimp. Mix Lobster Sauce into these ingredients and cook 5 minutes. Add brandy. Spoon this mixture onto pancakes. Roll and curve stuffed pancakes in the shape of a half moon. Sprinkle with Parmesan cheese, glaze and serve.

Serves: 4

Wine: Pouilly-Fuissé

Bingley Arms
Bardsey, Leeds, England
Chefs: Ian Walker and
   Christopher Haw

CHAMPAGNE SALMON PANCAKES

1½ cups crêpe batter (see index)
 2 tablespoons butter
 ¼ cup chopped onions
 ¼ cup chopped carrots
1½ cups dry champagne
 ½ teaspoon chopped parsley
 ¼ teaspoon marjoram
 ¼ teaspoon thyme
    Salt and freshly ground pepper to taste
 1 pound (500 grams) salmon (tail end)
1½ tablespoons flour
1¼ tablespoons butter
 ½ cup heavy cream
 ½ cup cooked asparagus spears

In an 8-inch crêpe pan (or shallow skillet) make four pancakes. Set aside. In a saucepan, melt butter and sauté first the onion and then the carrots about 3 minutes each. Stir in 1¼ cups champagne and simmer about 1 minute. Stir in parsley, marjoram, thyme, salt and freshly ground pepper. Poach salmon for about 15 minutes. Let cool in stock for another 15 minutes. Remove salmon from pan, reserving the liquid. Skin, fillet and flake the fish. Set aside and keep warm. Strain cooking liquid and reduce to about ¾ cup.

In another saucepan, make a roux with flour and butter. Pour in boiling reduced liquid, beating constantly. Warm cream and beat in by the spoonful; continue to simmer until sauce is thick. Reduce the remaining ¼ cup of champagne to about 1 tablespoon and add to sauce.

Fill each pancake with flaked salmon and fold over twice. Cover with cream sauce and garnish with asparagus.

Serves: 2

Sadko Restaurant

Leningrad, Soviet Union

BLINY A LA SUZDAL
(Crêpes with Salmon and Caviar)

 1 cup flour
 2 tablespoons sugar
 1 teaspoon active dry yeast
 4 egg whites
 ¾ cup milk
 ¼ cup butter
 2 tablespoons smoked salmon for each bliny
 2 tablespoons red or black caviar for each bliny
    Sour cream

Combine flour, sugar and dry yeast. Add egg whites and milk all at once and beat to make a smooth batter. Melt butter in a medium-sized skillet. When the skillet is quite hot, pour a small amount of batter in and tip pan to spread batter all over hot surface. Turn when bottom is brown and top of cake is almost dry. Fill bliny with salmon and/or caviar. Roll each into a cylinder. Top with sour cream.

Serves: 2

Wine: Tokay grape

Sadko Restaurant

Leningrad, Soviet Union

TURKEY, TONGUE OR HAM PANCAKES

Pancakes

1 cup flour
1 teaspoon salt
4 egg whites
¾ cup milk
Butter

Sift flour and salt. Add egg whites and milk all at once. Beat with a wire whisk or rotary beater until batter is smooth. Melt a small amount of butter in a small skillet. When skillet is quite hot, pour in about ¼ cup batter. Turn the pancake when bubbles show on the top. The second side will take less time to cook than the first. Add more butter, if necessary, to cook next cake. Keep finished pancakes warm until ready to fill.

Filling

1 tablespoon cranberries or cowberries
1 tablespoon slivered lemon or orange peel
Butter
½ cup chopped cooked turkey, ham or tongue

Sauté cranberries or cowberries along with slivered peel in butter until the berries are puffed and tender. Add chopped meat to skillet to heat through. Reserve.

Madeira Sauce

2 tablespoons butter
2 tablespoons minced shallots or scallions
1 tablespoon flour
1½ cups brown stock or consommé
2 tablespoons lemon juice
¼ cup Madeira

Melt butter in heavy saucepan or skillet. Sauté shallots very gently for about 5 minutes. Sprinkle flour over pan and stir to mix thoroughly. Add stock or consommé and lemon juice gradually, stirring constantly. When liquid boils, add wine and simmer for another 5 minutes.

Conclusion

½ cup sliced mushrooms
Butter

Sauté mushrooms gently in butter until cooked through. Fill pancakes with meat-berry-peel mixture and fold once. Top with Madeira Sauce and decorate with mushroom slices.

Serves: 2

Le Vert Galant

Paris, France

Chef: Garnier

SOUFFLE DE BARBUE

(Brill Soufflé)

2¼ pounds (1.25 kilogram) filleted brill or gray
   or lemon sole, bones reserved
 ½ cup chopped onion
 1 cup dry white wine
 ¼ cup parsley stems
 ¼ cup thyme
 1 teaspoon salt
 2 cups milk
 5 tablespoons flour
 5 tablespoons butter
 8 egg whites

Brown fish bones and onion in a casserole; then pour the white wine over them. Add 4 cups water, parsley stems, thyme and salt. Boil 20 minutes. Strain.

Reduce fish stock until only about ½ inch remains in bottom of a large saucepan. Cut the fillets into small pieces and add. Add milk. Let fish poach gently until it flakes easily.

Make a roux of flour and butter. Add roux bit by bit to fish and stock to form a thick sauce. Allow to cool to lukewarm. Beat egg whites until stiff. Carefully fold them into the prepared mixture. Pour into a floured soufflé dish and bake in a moderate (350° F.) oven for about 30 minutes. Test for doneness—the soufflé should be fairly firm. Serve with Hollandaise Sauce.

Hollandaise Sauce

 8 egg yolks
 ¼ cup lemon juice
 1 cup butter
   Salt and freshly ground white pepper to
   taste

Place egg yolks in the top of a double boiler. Make sure the water beneath never boils and that it does not touch the bottom of the upper pan. Beat in lemon juice and ¼ cup water with a wire whisk. Cut butter in small pieces and add, a few at a time, beating constantly. Add salt and pepper to taste. By the time the last bit of butter has been absorbed, the sauce should be thickened and ready to serve. If the sauce becomes too thick, beat in a tablespoon or two of *hot* water.

Serves: 4

Hôtel Plaza Athénée

Paris, France

Chef: Jean Plet

SOUFFLE DE HOMARD PLAZA ATHENEE

(Lobster Soufflé)

      3 2-pound (1-kilogram) lobsters
      2 tablespoons butter
      1 medium carrot, chopped
      2 tablespoons chopped onion
      1 tablespoon chopped chives
      1 tablespoon chopped parsley stems
         Salt and freshly ground pepper to taste
      1 teaspoon paprika
      2 tablespoons cognac
    ½ cup dry white wine
    ½ cup heavy cream
      3 tablespoons heavy cream
      2 tablespoons cognac
    ¼ cup butter
    ½ cup flour
    ½ cup hot milk
    ½ teaspoon salt
         Cayenne
      5 egg yolks
    ¾ cup finely grated Swiss or Parmesan cheese
      6 egg whites, stiffly beaten

Remove the claws from lobsters; cut the body sections into three or four pieces. In a saucepan large enough to hold the cut-up lobsters, melt 2 tablespoons butter. Add the carrot, onion and chives. Cook this mirepoix very slowly until the vegetables are soft but not brown. Add parsley.

Sprinkle lobsters with a little salt and pepper. Cook in a skillet over a brisk fire about 5 minutes, or until the lobster pieces are red on all sides. Place the lobsters on the mirepoix of vegetables and sprinkle with paprika. Add 2 tablespoons cognac, the wine and ½ cup cream; mix lightly. Bring to a boil and cook for 18 minutes, or until lobster meat is done.

Remove the lobsters from the pan, separate the meat from the shells and cut the meat into ¼-inch slices. Cook the liquid remaining in the pan until it is reduced to about half; add the remaining heavy cream and 2 tablespoons cognac. Strain, making sure all the fine bits of shell are removed. Add half the sauce to the sliced lobster meat, and keep the remaining sauce warm. Butter two 1-quart soufflé molds and divide the lobster mixture between them.

In a saucepan melt ¼ cup butter. Add flour and cook, stirring, until the roux turns golden. Stir hot milk in gradually and cook for 5 minutes, whisking constantly. Season with salt and a little cayenne. Beat egg yolks until light and stir into the hot sauce. Bring the sauce almost to a boil, stirring briskly. Fold in Swiss or Parmesan cheese, and cool. Fold in egg whites.

Cover the lobster in the two soufflé dishes with this cheese soufflé mixture. Bake the soufflés in a hot (400° F.) oven for 18 to 20 minutes, or until they are puffed and golden brown. Serve the reserved sauce separately.

Serves: 6

Wine: **Clément Blanc or Traminer Resérve de Grande Lignée**

Restaurant Operäkallaren
Stockholm, Sweden
Chef: Werner Vogeli

SOUFFLE DE SAUMON A L'OPRIS
(Salmon Soufflé)

> 1 pound (500 grams) fresh salmon
> 2 egg whites
> ½ teaspoon salt
> 4 cups whipped cream
> Sauce (recipe follows)

Mince salmon meat finely by running through food mill four or five times. Reserve head and trimmings for sauce. Mix meat with unbeaten egg whites and salt. Freeze for about ½ hour. Gradually add cream to mixture, stirring with a wooden spoon. All of cream may not be needed. The mixture should be firm, yet flexible. Pour into a buttered soufflé dish and set in a pan of water. Bake 35 to 40 minutes in a hot (400° F.) oven. During baking, cover with foil after 5 to 10 minutes to prevent surface from becoming too dark.

Sauce

> Salmon trimmings
> ¼ cup chopped carrot
> ¼ cup chopped onion
> 1 teaspoon thyme
> 1 bay leaf
> ¼ cup chopped shallots
> 2 parsley stalks
> Freshly ground white pepper
> 1½ cups red wine
> ¼ cup butter
> ¼ cup flour
> 1 cup meat extract
> 1 teaspoon lemon juice
> 1 cup small whole mushrooms, broiled

Cut salmon head and bones into small pieces and simmer in water to cover with carrot, onion, thyme, bay leaf, shallots, parsley stalks and white pepper. Then add red wine to the stock. Blend butter and flour and add to sauce to thicken. Strain; add meat extract and lemon juice. Finally, add mushrooms to sauce.

Serves: 4

Restaurant Riche
Stockholm, Sweden
Chef: Gunnar Schyl

SOUFFLE DE FROMAGE PRINCESSE BIRGITTA
(Swiss Cheese Soufflé)

> ¾ cup heavy cream
> 2 eggs, separated
> 6 tablespoons grated Parmesan cheese
> 3 tablespoons grated Swiss cheese
> 2 tablespoons brandy
> Salt
> Pinch cayenne
> Grated Parmesan cheese

Whip cream, not too stiff. Mix in egg yolks, cheeses, brandy, salt and cayenne. Beat egg whites and add. Butter and sprinkle with additional grated Parmesan four individual soufflé pots and fill almost to brim with cheese mixture. Put more grated cheese on top and bake in a moderately hot (375° F.) oven for 8 to 10 minutes. Serve immediately. As there is no flour in mixture, the soufflé will not stay puffed many minutes after it has left the oven.

Serves: 4

ESSO MOTOR HOTEL
Amsterdam, Netherlands
Chef: S. Tolsma
Fillet of Halibut "Lafayette"
(page 136)

ROYAL HOTEL
Copenhagen, Denmark
Chef: Mogens Bech Andersen
Roast Pork with Cracklings
(page 115)

THE BARRIE GRILL
KENSINGTON PALACE HOTEL
London, England
Chef: Larry Stove
Fillet of Beef Wellington
(page 80)

Section Ten

DESSERTS

Restaurant Gundel
Budapest, Hungary
Chef: Julius Pár

SOMLO

(Dessert Dumplings)

¼ cup sugar
½ cup flour
¼ cup ground walnuts
3 eggs
2 tablespoons crème de cacao
¼ cup dark rum
2 tablespoons finely chopped raisins
2 tablespoons finely chopped walnuts
½ cup heavy cream, whipped
Filling (recipe follows)
Chocolate Icing (recipe follows)

Sift sugar and flour together. Mix in ground walnuts. Beat eggs. Stir in crème de cacao. Add to dry ingredients. Form dough into six ladyfinger-shaped cookies and bake on a greased cookie sheet in a very slow (200° F.) oven until dry, about 30 minutes. Let cool completely.

Moisten walnut cookies with mixture of rum and ¼ cup water. Sprinkle with finely chopped raisins and walnuts. Spread prepared cooled filling on the cookies and refrigerate.

At serving time, place each cookie on a small plate. Dribble prepared Chocolate Icing over each one and decorate with unsweetened whipped cream.

Filling

½ cup milk
1 tablespoon flour
2 tablespoons vanilla sugar
3 tablespoons sugar
1 egg

Heat milk to scalding. Mix flour into sugars. Beat egg and add sugar mixture. Beat a little of the hot milk into egg mixture; then add to milk. Cook over hot, not boiling, water until custard thickens to the consistency of mayonnaise. Cool.

Chocolate Icing

3 tablespoons sugar
2 tablespoons water
1½ tablespoons crème de cacao
1 tablespoon rum

Boil sugar and water together to form a fairly heavy syrup; cool slightly and add crème de cacao and rum. Cool completely before using.

Serves: 6

Wine: White Tokay

Hotel International

Varna, Bulgaria

Chef: Stefan Kotarov

TART "INTERNATIONAL"

Cake

   8 eggs
1½ cups sugar
   2 cups cake flour
½ cup butter, melted and cooled
1½ tablespoons cocoa
½ cup almond meal*

Butter and flour three 8-inch springform cake pans. Have eggs at room temperature. In a very large bowl begin beating the eggs with an electric mixer. When foamy, add sugar and continue beating until mixture is very thick and forms a ribbon when beaters are lifted. Sift flour twice and add to batter in three parts. Fold in lightly. When almost all the flour has been mixed in, pour in butter and mix very gently. Pour one-third of batter into a cake pan and set aside. Divide remaining batter in half. Sift cocoa into one portion; add almond meal to the other. Mix gently as before and pour into the other two pans. Bake about 30 minutes in a moderate (350° F.) oven. Cool in pans for 10 minutes; then turn out on working surface and cool completely.

Filling

   4 eggs
   1 cup sugar
1½ cups unsalted butter, softened
   1 teaspoon vanilla extract
½ cup slivered almonds

Separate eggs. Reserve egg whites. Beat egg yolks with sugar until sugar dissolves and the mixture is light yellow and somewhat thick. Put over hot, not boiling, water and cook, beating constantly. (A hand electric mixer makes this step easy.) Continue beating and cooking until mixture is very thick. It should form a broad ribbon when dropped from a spoon. This step will take about 20 minutes. Do not let water boil!

Pour egg-sugar custard into the large bowl of a stationary mixer. Let it cool until it is comfortable to the touch. Start mixer at medium speed. When custard is just lukewarm, begin adding pieces of the butter. Continue beating at high speed until custard is completely cold and all butter incorporated. Stir vanilla extract into cooled custard.

Beat egg whites until they form soft shiny peaks. Do not overbeat. Put a large spoonful of the egg whites into the custard and mix thoroughly. Then pour custard mixture over egg whites and mix very gently. The filling should be very thick. It may be chilled for several hours to make it easier to handle. Stir in almonds just before assembling the cake.

Icing

4 squares dark semisweet chocolate
3 tablespoons almond liqueur
4 tablespoons unsalted butter
  Marzipan

Melt chocolate in liqueur in a double boiler. Add butter in small pieces. If icing is too soft, beat over iced water to thicken a bit. Reserve marzipan for garnishing finished cake.

Conclusion

Split cake layers with a long sharp knife. Beginning with a cocoa layer, spread filling on each piece and stack, alternating cocoa, plain and almond layers. Frost cake with chocolate icing. Decorate with marzipan (the Grand International uses its emblem, of course; initials or a seasonal motif would be attractive at home). Store cake in the refrigerator if it is not to be used immediately. To serve, let stand at room temperature for about 20 minutes to let icing soften.

Serves: 16

*Available in some stores, or make your own from blanched almonds in a blender.

Wine: Iskra red

Le Berlioz
Paris, France
Chef: Jean Claude Musseau

TARTE TATIN
(Apple Tart)

1 cup sugar
⅔ cup butter
3¼ pounds (1.5- kilograms) small Golden Delicious apples
  Shortbread (recipe follows)

Cook sugar and butter until sugar melts and turns golden. Peel and core apples and cut them in half; arrange them in a buttered heatproof mold. Pour caramel over apples and cook gently over a low flame until they are almost tender. Top mold with shortbread dough and bake in a hot (425° F.) oven for about 20 minutes, or until shortbread is done and lightly browned. To serve, invert mold on a platter that has low sides (in case caramel runs). Serve hot.

Shortbread

1¼ cups flour
½ cup sugar
½ teaspoon salt
⅔ cup butter
1 egg, beaten

Sift dry ingredients together. Cut in butter. Mix in egg, stirring as little as possible.

Serves: 8

Wine: Quincy blanc Vuis de la Laire

Hotel Lev

Ljubljana, Yugoslavia

Djoni Perdan

SLOVENIAN STRUKLJU

(Boiled Cheese Rolls)

Pastry

    1 tablespoon yeast
    1 teaspoon sugar
    1 egg, beaten
    ¼ teaspoon salt
    1½ tablespoons oil
    1¼ cups flour

Dissolve yeast and sugar in 2 cups warm water in a large bowl. Stir in egg, salt and oil. Blend in flour until completely mixed. Knead for about 2 minutes. Cover bowl with a damp cloth and set in a warm place to rise for 30 minutes.

Filling

    ½ cup butter
    1 cup sugar
    3 eggs
    1 teaspoon vanilla extract
    3 cups cottage cheese
    ¼ cup raisins
    ½ cup sour cream

Cream butter and sugar together. Beat in eggs until mixture is pale and fluffy. Stir in vanilla extract, cottage cheese, raisins and sour cream. Set aside.

Topping

    7 tablespoons sugar
    3½ tablespoons bread crumbs
    3½ tablespoons butter, melted

Thoroughly mix all the above ingredients. Set aside.

Conclusion

Roll out pastry to ¾-inch thickness. Spread on filling and roll into a log about 4 inches thick and 19 inches long. Wrap log in a cloth, securing the ends with string, and boil for 40 minutes in water to cover. Place on a heatproof dish, remove cloth, sprinkle on the topping and bake in a very hot (450° F.) oven for about 5 minutes, or until topping is brown. Cut into pieces ½-inch thick and serve on wooden plates.

Serves: 10

Wine: Ljutomer

The Russell
Dublin, Ireland
Chef: Tony Butler

LE CROQUEMBOUCHE

(Pastry Tower)

Filled Pastry

    1 cup butter
       Pinch salt
       Pinch sugar
 1½ cups flour
    8 eggs
  ½ cup heavy cream, whipped
    2 tablespoons rum

Bring butter, 1 cup water, salt and sugar to a boil. Add flour all at once, stirring briskly, and remove from heat. Beat until batter forms a ball. Add eggs, one at a time, beating well after each addition. Pipe from a pastry bag onto an ungreased baking sheet to form small puffs. Bake in a hot (400° F.) oven until golden and puffed. Slit and remove soft centers; turn off oven and return puffs to dry out a few minutes. Combine whipped cream with rum. When puffs are cool, fill with the whipped cream mixture.

Nougatine

    2 cups sugar
    2 cups chopped almonds
    1 teaspoon salad (not olive) oil

Cook sugar and ¾ cup water until a very thick dark syrup is formed. Add almonds and pour onto a cold slab of oiled marble or metal. When cool enough to handle, reserve a small portion and shape the rest into a cone. Make several fancy shapes—stars or flowers—from the reserved nougatine.

Caramel

1¼ cups sugar

Boil sugar and ½ cup water together until a thick dark syrup forms.

Conclusion

Place cooled nougatine cone large end down on a large platter. One by one dip the filled puffs in the caramel syrup (reheat it if it gets too stiff) and place around the nougatine close to each other, round sides out, to build a pyramid. Finally, decorate with pieces of shaped nougatine. Assemble the croquembouche as near as possible to serving time since the cream-filled puffs are very, very perishable and refrigeration would spoil the texture of the puffs.

Serves: 8

Wine: Château la Faite 1960

Churchill Hotel

London, England

PARIS BRESSE
(Cream-Filled Pastry Ring)

Pâte à Chou

¼ cup butter
½ cup flour
4 eggs
¼ cup slivered almonds

Boil ½ cup water and butter together. When butter is melted, add all the flour at once and beat until smooth. Beat in the eggs one at a time, continuing to beat until mixture is smooth and creamy. Lightly butter a 12-inch round heatproof tray. Put pâte à chou into a pastry bag and pipe around the edge of tray, forming a thick ring of pastry. Sprinkle with almonds and bake in a hot (400° F.) oven for 20 minutes.

Crème Pâtissière

3 egg yolks
½ cup sugar
¼ cup flour
1¼ cups milk
¼ teaspoon vanilla extract

Beat egg yolks until light. Gradually add sugar and beat until mixture forms a ribbon when lifted from the beater. Add the flour and blend thoroughly. In a separate saucepan, boil milk and vanilla extract together. Add half of the vanilla milk to the batter and stir rapidly. Return this mixture to the remaining milk and bring to a boil, beating rapidly and continuously until thoroughly blended.

Crème Chantilly

1¼ cups heavy cream
2 tablespoons sugar

Beat cream and sugar together until mixture is fluffy.

Conclusion

Baked pastry ring
Crème Pâtissière
Crème Chantilly
½ cup whole strawberries
6 pineapple ring halves
Powdered sugar

Cut pastry ring in half, horizontally. Place bottom half on a serving dish. Mix half of the Crème Pâtissière with half of the Crème Chantilly. Place this in a pastry bag. Pipe onto lower half of ring. Place top half of the ring on the bottom half. Refill the pastry bag with remaining Crème Pâtissière and Crème Chantilly. Pipe ten rosettes around the top of the ring. Decorate with whole strawberries placed on each rosette and pineapple slices between rosettes. Sprinkle powdered sugar over all.

Serves: 6

Wine: Château d'Yquem 1961

Royal Vézère

Le Bugue, France

Chef: Christian Rouffignac

GATEAU GLACE AUX NOIX
(Iced Walnut Cake)

Sponge Cake

> 4 eggs
> ½ cup sugar
> 1 teaspoon vanilla extract
> ¾ cup flour, sifted
> ½ cup butter, melted and cooled

Beat eggs and sugar together until the mixture is light-colored. Cook over hot, not boiling, water, beating constantly, until thick. This will take about 20 minutes. (An electric hand-mixer makes the process much easier.)

When the egg-sugar mixture is very thick, remove from heat. Add vanilla extract. Carefully fold in the flour. When it has been incorporated, stir in the butter. Pour batter into a buttered and floured 8-inch cake pan and bake for 30 minutes in a moderate (350° F.) oven. When the cake is done, cool in the pan for 10 minutes; then turn out on working surface to cool completely.

Filling

> 4 egg yolks
> ¾ cup sugar
> ⅔ cup milk, scalded
> 1 cup cold unsalted butter
> 1 teaspoon vanilla extract

Beat egg yolks and sugar until mixture is thickened slightly and a light color. Beat in the hot milk in a very fine stream. Cook custard over hot, not boiling, water until it is thick enough to coat a spoon. Remove from heat and beat hard for a minute or two to cool somewhat. Cut the butter into small pieces. Add to custard, still beating constantly, a few pieces at a time, until all the butter is incorporated. The mixture should be thick and glossy. Stir in vanilla extract.

Conclusion

> ¼ cup kirsch
> 2 cups tutti frutti ice cream
> 1¼ cups walnuts

Split sponge cake into two layers. Sprinkle with kirsch. Assemble cake—a layer of sponge, a layer of filling, the ice cream, a layer of walnuts, another layer of filling, second layer of sponge. Frost the whole cake with the filling and decorate with walnuts. Put the cake in the freezer until 5 minutes before serving time.

Serves: 6

Wine: Monbazillac

Capucin Gourmand

Nancy, France

Chef: Maître Jean

GATEAU DOMINIQUE

(Cake Dominique)

½ cup butter
½ cup sugar
2 eggs
2 teaspoons baking powder
1 teaspoon finely ground almond powder
½ cup flour
2 tablespoons raisins (sultanas), soaked in rum

Let the butter soften in a bowl; then mix well with the sugar. Add one whole egg, mix again; add the other egg, mix again. Sift the baking powder with the almond powder and the flour. Finally fold in the soaked raisins.

Butter a 1½-quart mold and line bottom with buttered white paper. Pour the batter carefully into the mold and bake 30 minutes in a moderately slow (325° F.) oven.

Serves: 4

Wine: Sauterne or Gewurtztraminer

Hotel National

Moscow, Soviet Union

ICE CREAM FLAN

Pastry

½ cup butter
1 cup flour
½ teaspoon salt
2 or 3 tablespoons ice water

Cut butter into flour with a pastry blender or two table knives. When the mixture resembles coarse cornmeal, add salt and then water, a tablespoon at a time. Use no more water than is necessary for dough to hold together. Roll pastry thin and line two tart dishes. Bake until golden brown, about 10 minutes, in a hot (400° F.) oven.

Filling

2 tablespoons strawberry jam
1 cup canned fruit, well drained
2 egg whites
¼ cup powdered sugar
⅔ cup ice cream (2 good-sized scoops)

To serve, spread jam in baked and cooled pastry shells. Add fruit. Beat egg whites with sugar to form a stiff meringue. Gently mix ice cream into meringue and top tarts with the mixture. Serve immediately.

Serves: 2

Pierre
Pau, France
Chef: Roland Casau

LE GATEAU DES PRELATS

(Cake with Chocolate Mousse)

     2 cups sugar
     5 eggs
    15 egg yolks
    3½ ounces baking chocolate, melted
     2 cups heavy cream, whipped
    12 ladyfingers or 1 layer sponge cake, thinly
        sliced
    ¼ cup strong coffee
        Additional melted chocolate (optional)
        Brandied cherries (optional)
        Candied orange peel (optional)

Cook sugar and a scant ½ cup water until syrup forms a thin thread from end of spoon to pan. Cool syrup somewhat (about 200° F. on a candy thermometer). Add whole eggs and egg yolks, beating well with a wire whisk (you may find an electric mixer more satisfactory) until the mixture is completely cool. Add melted chocolate and mix thoroughly. Fold in whipped cream. Set aside.

Line a rectangular 2½-quart mold with some of the split ladyfingers or sponge-cake slices. Sprinkle with strong coffee. Spread chocolate mixture into mold and cover top with remaining ladyfingers or cake slices. Cover mold with waxed paper and refrigerate for 24 hours.

Unmold on a silver plate; pour more melted bitter chocolate over gâteau as a garnish, if desired. Flavor is also improved by decorating the mold with cherries soaked in brandy or with candied orange peel.

Serves: 8

Restaurant de la Mère Guy
Lyon, France
Chef: Roger Roucou

MARJOLAINE GLACE AU CHOCOLAT

(Chocolate Ice Cream "Marjolaine")

    2 cups slivered almonds
    2 cups sugar
    2 cups melted butter
    4 eggs
    4 egg yolks
    1 cup chocolate ice cream
    2 tablespoons vanilla sugar

Crush almonds in a pestle and add sugar, melted butter, eggs and egg yolks, to make a rather compact batter. Spread it on a pastry board and roll out to 1 inch in thickness. Bake in a very slow (220° F.) oven until dry and light brown, about 1½ hours. Let cool.

Cut almond pastry in half. Place one layer on top of the other with chocolate ice cream in between. Store in freezer until 10 minutes before serving. Sprinkle with vanilla sugar before serving.

Serves: 4

Wine: Roederer 1964

Fouquet's

Paris, France

Chef: André Fevre

SOUFFLE GLACE FRAMBOISINE

(Frozen Raspberry Soufflé)

½ cup raspberry juice
½ cup sugar
4 egg yolks
1⅔ cups heavy cream
6 tablespoons milk
1 tablespoon raspberry liquor
½ cup heavy cream, whipped
½ cup fresh raspberries

Boil the raspberry juice with the sugar to make a syrup. Add the egg yolks; beat well with wire whisk. Let cool.

Beat the cream and the milk until softly whipped. Add the raspberry liquor and syrup-egg mixture and blend gently. Put this mixture into a soufflé dish and place it in the freezer for 6 hours.

Before serving, decorate the soufflé with whipped cream and raspberries.

Serves: 6

Wine: Champagne Brut

Hotel Pension Schwarzenberg

Vienna, Austria

SCHMANKERLBOMBE

(Bavarian Cream Mold)

Schmankerl

½ cup milk
1 cup flour
½ cup sugar
1 tablespoon butter

Make a thick paste from milk and flour; add sugar. Butter baking sheet and spread the paste *very* thinly on it with a spatula. (It should be thin enough to read through.) Place in a slow (250° F.) oven and bake until brown. Remove the Schmankerl from the pan and, when cold, break into small pieces.

Conclusion

1 cup heavy cream, whipped
1 cup Bavarian cream
1 cup strawberry sauce

Blend the whipped cream, Bavarian cream and pieces of Schmankerl together, and put into a large charlotte mold. Allow the filled mold to remain in the freezer for at least 3 hours. Serve with strawberry sauce, preferably homemade. (Two cups fresh or frozen strawberries boiled in ½ cup water with ½ cup sugar. Sieve and chill.)

Serves: 4

Rôtisserie des Cordeliers
Nancy, France
Chef: M. Antoine

MIRABELLE SURPRISE DES CORDELIERS
(Plum Ice Cream Meringue)

Macaroons

½ cup blanched almonds
1 cup sugar
2 egg whites
2 tablespoons sugar
2 tablespoons light corn syrup

Grind together almonds and 1 cup sugar. Add egg whites and grind again. Cook the 2 tablespoons sugar and syrup until it forms a large ball. Add the sugar-almond-egg mixture. Place batter in pastry bag and squeeze out little round macaroons on moistened paper. Bake in a slow (250° F.) oven until dry and lightly browned.

Ice Cream

1 cup Mirabelle plums*
½ cup plum brandy
4 cups milk
6 egg yolks
1¼ cups sugar

Soak the plums in the plum brandy for several hours. Drain, reserving brandy. Mix milk, egg yolks and sugar. To avoid crushing the plums, add them when the mixture has been almost entirely blended. Pour the ice cream mixture into a round mold, placing macaroons on top. Freeze until very firm.

Meringue

8 egg whites
4½ cups sugar
2½ cups almonds, crushed

Beat egg whites until frothy; add sugar and continue beating until very stiff. Sift almonds and blend in.

Conclusion

½ cup chopped almonds
¼ cup sugar

Unmold ice cream onto a round serving dish. Over it pipe the meringue, using a pastry bag. Sprinkle chopped almonds over it and sugar to glaze. Place under broiler until lightly caramelized. Flame with reserved plum brandy.

Serves: 10

*Small French plums also available canned.

Wine: Champagne Florens Louis 1964 (Piper Heidsick)

Brown's Hotel

London, England

Chef: Peter Morton

COURONNE D'ANANAS MARIETTE

(Crown of Pineapple)

>   Glazing Syrup (recipe follows)
> 1 large fresh pineapple
> ½ cup orange sherbet
> ½ cup lemon sherbet
> 1 cup praline ice cream
> ½ cup fresh raspberries
> ½ cup fresh strawberries
>   Meringue à la Swiss (recipe follows)
> 3 fresh peaches, peeled and halved
>   Langues de Chat (recipe follows)

Cut pineapple lengthwise. Scoop out the flesh, chop and set aside. Glaze the pineapple half-shells with Glazing Syrup. Fill half-shells with scoops of orange sherbet, lemon sherbet, praline ice cream, chopped pineapple, raspberries and strawberries. Cover with Meringue à la Swiss. Glaze peach halves with Glazing Syrup and use to garnish. Stud with Langues de Chat to resemble a crown.

Meringue à la Swiss

> 4 egg whites
> 1 cup powdered sugar
> 1 tablespoon crème de menthe

Beat egg whites and powdered sugar over boiling water until stiff. Slowly beat in crème de menthe.

Glazing Syrup

> 1 cup sugar

Boil sugar and ⅓ cup water together until a little beyond the soft ball stage, or 244° F. on a candy thermometer. Coat the peaches and pineapple shells with the glaze and refrigerate until thoroughly chilled.

Langues de Chat*

> ¼ cup butter, softened
> ⅓ cup sugar
> 1 lemon peel, grated
> 2 or 3 egg whites (to make ¼ cup)
> ⅓ cup flour

Beat together butter, sugar and lemon peel in a mixing bowl. When pale and fluffy, pour in egg whites and blend lightly. Gradually sift and stir the flour into the batter.

Lightly butter and dust with flour two baking sheets. Using a saucer or other round object, mark off four circles about 5½ inches in diameter on each sheet. Lightly oil two large cups or small bowls about 4 inches in diameter at the top, 2 inches at the bottom and 2½ inches deep. Set aside. Place a tablespoon of batter into each circle on the cookie sheets and spread to about 1/16-inch thickness. Bake in a very hot (450° F.) oven for 5 minutes, or until cookies have browned lightly to within about an inch of their centers. Remove cookies with a flexible spatula and turn over an oiled cup or bowl. With your fingers, press cookie against the bowl. Repeat procedure with each cookie, removing crisped cookies after each initial step. Bake one sheet of cookies at a time.

Serves: 4 or 6

*This batter makes eight 3½-inch Langues de Chat. They can be frozen and kept indefinitely.

Wine: Bollinger 1964 or other dry champagne

Belle Avenue

Göteborg, Sweden

Chef: Allan Hult

BLACK CURRANT SHERBET BELLE AVENUE

    4 cups sugar
       Juice of 4 lemons
    4 lemon peels
    ¼ cup black currant juice
    2 cups light cream
       Nut Ring (recipe follows)
    1 cup rum

Bring 4 cups water, sugar, lemon juice and lemon peel to a boil. Strain through a cloth and flavor with black currant juice. Put in freezer. When sherbet is half frozen, stir in the cream. Serve the frozen sherbet in Nut Ring soaked with rum.

Nut Ring

    2 tablespoons butter
    ¼ cup sugar
    2 eggs, separated
    2 tablespoons grated nougat
    3 tablespoons grated almond

Whip the butter, add 2 tablespoons sugar and the egg yolks. Combine the nougat and almonds and mix in. Whip egg whites with the remaining 2 tablespoons sugar. Fold into egg-yolk mixture and pour into buttered and floured ring-shaped mold. Bake in a moderate (350° F.) oven for about 25 minutes.

Serves: 4

Rôtisserie des Cordeliers

Nancy, France

Chef: M. Antoine

SORBET VIEUX KIRSCH

(Kirsch Sherbet)

Sherbet

- 1 cup brandied cherries
- ¼ cup superfine sugar
- 2 tablespoons lemon juice
- 1 egg white
- 1 tablespoon kirsch

Reserve two whole cherries for decoration. Purée remaining cherries and add sugar and lemon juice; mix until sugar is completely dissolved. Beat egg white until it forms soft peaks. Fold in cherry mixture and kirsch. Turn into ice tray or freezer dish and freeze until firm. Stir several times during freezing to break up ice crystals.

Syrup

- ½ cup kirsch
- 2 cups sugar

Boil kirsch, ¼ cup water and sugar together until syrup forms a very soft ball in cold water.

Conclusion

To serve, place two scoops of sherbet in a dessert dish. Cover with syrup and decorate with a reserved brandied cherry rolled in superfine sugar.

Serves: 2

Tour Eiffel

Paris, France

Chef: Robert Saget

SURPRISE TOUR EIFFEL

(Meringue with Mirabelle Brandy)

- 1 cup sugar
- 2 egg yolks
- 1 teaspoon vanilla extract or 1 pulverized vanilla bean
- 4 ladyfingers or 4 slices sponge cake
- ¼ cup kirsch
- 8 scoops vanilla ice cream
- 12 egg whites
- ½ cup Mirabelle brandy

Make a paste with ½ cup sugar, egg yolks and vanilla extract or a bit of pulverized vanilla bean.

Soak ladyfingers or cake slices in kirsch. Top them with scoops of vanilla ice cream.

Beat egg whites to a stiff froth with ½ cup sugar; gently mix in egg-sugar paste. Keep beating until very stiff. Spread meringue on ice cream with a steel spatula, shaping each dessert like a baked Alaska. Reserve enough meringue to decorate, using a fluted tip on a pastry bag.

Bake in a very hot (450° F.) oven for about 5 minutes, or just until the meringue is browned. Before serving, pour Mirabelle brandy over baked desserts and ignite them. (A good tip to make rum or brandy flame: warm it first.)

Serves: 4

Wine: Champagne Perrier-Jouet 1964

Le Pavillon de l'Elysée
Paris, France
Chef: Jean Pibourdin

LE SOUFFLE DU PAVILLON

6 large oranges
½ cup diced candied fruit
6 tablespoons Grand Marnier
3 cups orange sherbet
6 egg whites
1 cup powdered sugar
4 candied cherries
2 tablespoons sugar

Cut a small slice from the top of each orange. Grate this peel. Remove the flesh of the oranges without damaging the peel. Soak the candied fruit in the Grand Marnier and put it in the bottom of the orange shells. Next add a scoop of very hard-frozen orange sherbet.

Beat the egg whites until very stiff; add sugar and the peel of the orange tops. Fill the orange shells, letting the filling lap decoratively over the edges. Top with the candied cherries; sprinkle with sugar and put in a very hot (450° F.) oven in a shallow baking dish just long enough for meringue to brown lightly. Serve immediately with cookies, if desired.

Serves: 6

Wine: Champagne

Gaston et Gastounette
Cannes, France
Chef: Daniel Rouvière

LE SECRET DES MOINES
(Monks' Secret)

½ cup egg whites (about 4)
½ cup powdered sugar, sifted
1 teaspoon vanilla extract
¾ cup cake flour
12 ladyfingers
½ cup Lerina or other liqueur
6 tablespoons chopped candied fruit
6 scoops vanilla ice cream
½ cup heavy cream, whipped and slightly sweetened
Bitter chocolate, slivered into curls
Candied cherries

Butter and flour a cookie sheet and set aside. Prepare a pastry bag with a fairly large plain tip.

Beat egg whites until foamy. Add sugar, beating after each spoonful until it is completely absorbed. Continue beating until egg whites stand in stiff shiny peaks. Blend in vanilla extract.

Sift flour twice. Add to meringue mixture in three parts, quickly and gently folding after each addition. Fill pastry bag and shape six cup-shaped pastries on the cookie sheet. Dry in a *very* slow (200° F.) oven for about 40 minutes. Cool completely. Break two ladyfingers into each cup. Moisten with liqueur. Add candied fruit, then scoop of ice cream. Top with whipped cream, chocolate curls and a cherry.

Serves: 6

Wine: Graves

The Caprice

London, England

Chef: Brian Cotterill

ANANAS A LA BELLE DE MEAUX
(Pineapple in Kirsch)

  1 large pineapple
  2 tablespoons kirsch
  ¼ cup sugar
  ½ cup heavy cream, whipped
  1 cup strawberries
    Sponge layer (optional)

Cut pineapple in half lengthwise, scoop out fruit and cut it into ½-inch cubes. To this add kirsch and sugar (taste here—pineapples vary greatly in sweetness). Replace this mixture in pineapple shell, cover with cream and decorate with strawberries, or serve fruit on a sponge-cake base filled with strawberries, if desired.

Serves: 6

Wine: Château d'Yquem, Sauternes 1966

Hotel International

Brno, Czechoslovakia

BAKED PEACH "INTERNATIONAL"

  1 tablespoon Curaçao
  5 sponge biscuits (ladyfingers)
  5 peaches, peeled and halved
  ¼ cup sliced bananas
1½ tablespoons toasted, crushed almonds
  1 tablespoon grated dark (bitter) chocolate
  1 tablespoon rum
  5 egg whites
  ⅔ cup sugar
  2 egg yolks, beaten
1½ tablespoons grated nuts
  2 teaspoons potato flour
  2 tablespoons sugar

Drop a little Curaçao on the sponge biscuits. Place them in a buttered heatproof dish. Arrange peach halves on top. Mix sliced bananas with almonds and chocolate. Put mixture on peach halves and sprinkle with rum. Beat egg whites until frothy; gradually add sugar and beat until stiff peaks are formed. Gently fold in egg yolks, nuts and flour. Spoon meringue over peaches. Sprinkle with sugar. Bake in a hot (400° F.) oven for about 10 minutes, or until meringue is lightly browned. Watch carefully to prevent burning.

Serves: 4

London Hilton
London, England
Chef: Oswald Mair

REAL PEACH MELBA

  4 peaches
  4 eggs
  2 cups milk, scalded
  1 cup sugar
  1 teaspoon vanilla extract
  1¼ cups heavy cream
  ½ cup raspberries, puréed

Scald peaches briefly in hot water; peel and split into halves.

Make an egg custard by adding eggs to scalded milk. Add sugar and vanilla extract. Remove custard from stove, cool and place it in the refrigerator to chill thoroughly. Then fold cream into the custard and store mixture in the coldest part of the refrigerator.

When custard is very cold and thick, place large spoonfuls in the bottom of four dessert dishes or champagne glasses. Place two peach halves on either side. Top with unsweetened raspberry purée.

Serves: 4

Wine: Champagne

Alcron
Prague, Czechoslovakia
Chef: M. Hribek

PEACH ALCRON

  3 cups fresh peach slices
  2 tablespoons lemon juice
  2 cups milk
  5 eggs, separated
  1½ cups powdered sugar
  10 ladyfingers, split lengthwise
  2 tablespoons Curaçao
  ¼ cup grated bitter chocolate
  ¼ cup cream, whipped
  ½ cup sugar
  ¼ cup slivered toasted almonds

Sprinkle peach slices with lemon juice to preserve fresh color.

Prepare custard by mixing milk, egg yolks and sugar in the top of a double boiler. Cook over hot, not boiling, water, stirring constantly, until custard thickens. Cool.

In a buttered heatproof serving dish arrange ladyfingers, split side down, in one layer. Sprinkle with Curaçao and grated chocolate. Place drained peach slices on ladyfinger base. Mix custard and whipped cream and pour over.

Beat egg whites until foamy. Add sugar a little at a time and continue beating until stiff and glossy. Spread over custard. Sprinkle with almonds. Place in a hot (400° F.) oven for about 10 minutes, or until meringue is lightly browned. Serve hot or chilled.

Serves: 10

Bristol

Warsaw, Poland

Le Coq d'Or

London, England

Chef: J. C. Besnier

GRUSZKA PO WARSZAWSKU

(Pears Warsaw)

- 10 pieces sponge cake
- Punch (recipe follows)
- 10 canned pear halves
- Apricot Sauce (recipe follows)
- 1 cup blanched almonds, grated

Soak each portion of sponge cake in punch; then put in a flat glass bowl and place a pear half on each piece of cake. Cover with Apricot Sauce and sprinkle with grated almonds.

Punch

- 1 cup sugar
- 1 tablespoon grated lemon peel
- 1 tablespoon grated orange peel
- ½ cup vodka
- ½ cup cognac
- 1 tablespoon rum

Bring 1 cup water to a boil. Add sugar, lemon peel, orange peel, vodka, cognac and rum to boiling water. Mix, cool and set aside 1 to 2 hours.

Apricot Sauce

- 2 cups canned apricots
- ½ cup sugar
- 1 tablespoon lemon juice
- ½ cup Madeira

Rub canned apricots through a sieve with a spoon. Add sugar, lemon juice and Madeira.

Serves: 4 to 6

LE SOUFFLE COQ D'OR

(Raspberry Soufflé)

- 4 tablespoons Crème Pâtissière (see index)
- 3 egg yolks
- 5 egg whites
- ½ cup raspberries
- ¼ cup kirsch
- 4 pieces génoise (sponge cake)

Combine Crème Pâtissière with egg yolks. Whisk egg whites into a firm froth and fold into mixture. Marinate raspberries in kirsch. Place raspberries on pieces of génoise in each of four individual soufflé molds and cover with the prepared egg mixture. Cook in a moderately slow (300° F.) oven for 15 minutes.

Serves: 4

Café Royal
Edinburgh, Scotland
Chef: William Marshall

DANISH PANCAKES

⅓ cup flour
½ cup sugar
2 eggs
2½ cups milk
3 egg yolks
½ teaspoon vanilla extract
3 tablespoons chopped almonds
¼ cup chopped glacé cherries
4 whole glacé cherries
¼ cup apricot jam
½ cup brandy
½ cup very heavy cream

Make eight pancakes using for the batter ¼ cup flour, 1 tablespoon sugar, 2 eggs and 1¼ cups milk.

For filling, beat 3 egg yolks, the remaining sugar, remaining flour and ½ teaspoon vanilla extract together in a saucepan. Heat 1¼ cups milk just to boiling. Add to egg mixture. Return to stove and cook gently for 2 minutes, stirring constantly. Mix in almonds and chopped glacé cherries.

Divide mixture into eight portions and spread on pancakes; roll. Arrange in serving dish. Boil apricot jam and brandy together and pour over pancakes. Garnish with cream and glacé cherries. Serve very hot.

Serves: 4

Restaurant Excelsior
Amsterdam, Netherlands
Chef: J. Dresscher

CREPES A LA FAÇON DU MAITRE

(Thin Pancakes in Hot Mocha Sauce)

4 thin delicate pancakes (see " Crêpes " in index)
¼ cup butter
¼ cup sugar
1 tablespoon strong mocha coffee
1 teaspoon crème de cacao
1 teaspoon brandy

Keep pancakes warm. Finish at the table. Cream butter and sugar and heat in a chafing dish. Add coffee and crème de cacao. Place the prepared pancakes in pan with sauce and flame with brandy.

Serves: 2

Le Grand Veneur

Paris, France

CREPES SOUFFLES

Crêpes

½ cup milk
4 eggs, separated
1 teaspoon vanilla extract
1 cup flour
¼ cup sugar
Butter

Beat milk, ½ cup water, egg yolks and vanilla extract together. Sift flour and sugar. Add liquid all at once and beat with a wire whisk until batter is smooth. Let batter rest at least 1 hour. When ready to cook crêpes, beat egg whites until they form stiff peaks. Carefully fold egg whites into batter. Cook very thin crêpes on both sides in a buttered crêpe pan or skillet. Fold cooked crêpes into quarters and place in chafing dish or heatproof serving dish. Keep warm.

Conclusion

2 tablespoons butter
2 tablespoons sugar
1 lemon peel, cut in fine slivers
1 orange peel, cut in fine slivers
¼ cup Cointreau
¼ cup cognac

Melt butter in a small pan. Add sugar and peels and cook gently for 5 minutes, stirring to prevent scorching. Add Cointreau and just heat through. Pour syrup over crêpes, flame with cognac and serve hot.

Serves: 6

Vinogradi

Belgrade, Yugoslavia

Chef: Zivan Miljus

PANCAKES "VINOGRADI"

Pancakes

  2 eggs
1½ tablespoons sugar
  1 tablespoon salt
  ½ cup flour

Beat eggs and sugar together. Add salt. Alternately, beat in flour and 1 cup water until completely mixed and smooth. Lightly oil a 6-inch skillet and fry pancakes, using about ¼ cup of batter for each. Set aside.

Filling

  ½ cup chopped nuts (walnuts, filberts, etc.)
1½ tablespoons sugar
1½ tablespoons raisins
  ¼ cup rum

Mix dry ingredients and sprinkle with rum until mixture is moist and of spreading consistency. Set aside.

Chateau (topping)

  2 egg yolks, beaten
10 tablespoons sugar
  2 teaspoons vanilla extract
  ½ cup heavy cream, boiling

In a saucepan beat egg yolks and sugar together over a low flame until mixture is smooth and creamy. Stir in vanilla extract. Beat the cream in gradually until the sauce is as thick as custard. Set aside.

Conclusion

Spread filling on each pancake and roll, pressing the edges together. Place rolled pancakes in a deep heatproof serving dish and pour topping over them. Bake in a very hot (475° F.) oven for about 5 minutes. Watch carefully so that custard sauce does not curdle.

Serves: 4

Hunting Lodge

London, England

Chef: H. P. Lullier

PORT WINE SYLLABUB

  1 cup heavy cream
  1 teaspoon lemon juice
  1 cup sugar
  ½ cup port
  2 egg whites

Whip cream with lemon juice and sugar. Mix port with egg whites. Combine mixtures and blend. Chill. Serve with short cookies, if desired.

Serves: 6

Royal Hotel
Copenhagen, Denmark
Chef: O. Tolstrup

CORBEILLE "ROYAL"

(Meringue Baskets)

2 egg whites
½ cup sugar
½ cup semisweet chocolate
½ cup broken, roasted nuts
2 tablespoons coffee liqueur
1 teaspoon instant coffee
¼ cup heavy cream, whipped

Beat egg whites until foamy. Add sugar gradually, beating well after each addition until all sugar is dissolved. Continue beating until meringue is very stiff and shiny. Form into a basket shape on damp brown paper on a cookie sheet. Dry in a slow (250° F.) oven until firm but not browned.

Melt chocolate and pour out on a buttered cookie sheet or plate. While still soft, cut a circle the size of the meringue basket with a cookie cutter. Also cut a strip long enough to become the "handle" of the basket. Let cool but do not chill.

Add liqueur and instant coffee to whipped cream and blend in gently.

To assemble, place chocolate round on serving plate. Place meringue basket on top of chocolate. Sprinkle meringue with nuts, reserving some, and fill the basket with the flavored whipped cream. Attach the chocolate "handle" and sprinkle all with reserved nuts.

Serves: 1

London Hilton
London, England
Chef: Oswald Mair

SNOWBALLS

6 eggs, separated
1 cup sugar
2½ cups milk
¼ cup sugar
1 teaspoon vanilla extract

Beat egg whites with 1 cup sugar to make a stiff glossy meringue. Form into six or eight round meringues and poach in barely simmering water until firm. Turn meringues to poach evenly. Remove with a slotted spoon and drain well. Place in a large serving bowl and chill.

Scald milk—it must not boil—then beat in egg yolks, ¼ cup sugar and vanilla extract. Bring to just below boiling point. Allow to get cold, and then pour over snowballs. Serve very cold.

Serves: 6 or 8

Lapérouse

Paris, France

Chef: Fernand Poisson

SOUFFLE LAPEROUSE

12 eggs

1½ cups sugar

⅔ cup sifted flour

4 cups milk

1 vanilla bean

1 cup caramelized sugar

2 tablespoons rum

⅔ cup candied fruit

   Sugar

Separate the eggs; mix the yolks with the sugar and sifted flour.

Bring milk to a boil with a vanilla bean. When milk starts to boil, stir the egg-yolk mixture into it. Beat very well to make a smooth batter. Bring the batter to a rolling boil again and set it aside immediately. To this batter add the caramelized sugar, rum and candied fruit.

Beat the egg whites until they form stiff, shiny peaks and fold them into the batter.

Butter and sprinkle a large soufflé dish with sugar. Place soufflé in a moderate (350° F.) oven for about 20 minutes. Soufflé should be fairly firm when done.

When ready to serve, sprinkle some sugar over the soufflé and let the top caramelize quickly under the broiler. The top of the soufflé may also be pricked a little and moistened with additional rum, if desired.

Serves: 12

Grand Sofia

Sofia, Bulgaria

Chef: Velko Pavlov

BULGARIAN CREAM

1½ tablespoons unflavored gelatin

1¼ cups milk

4 egg yolks

1 cup sugar

2 teaspoons vanilla extract

1 tablespoon liqueur

1 tablespoon rum

½ cup jam

¼ cup macaroon crumbs

1 cup heavy cream

1 cup whipped cream

⅔ cup chocolate sauce

Soften gelatin in 3 tablespoons cold water. Beat together milk, egg yolks, sugar and softened gelatin. Heat to boiling point, but do not allow to boil. Strain and cool until slightly set. Stir in the vanilla, liqueur, rum, jam, macaroon crumbs and cream. Pour into individual molds and cool. Serve decorated with whipped cream and chocolate sauce.

Serves: 5

Index

Restaurants and Locations